The Rhapsodes

D0888779

Bordwell, David,
The Rhapsodes : how
1940s critics changed A
2016.
33305236485813
cu   08/12/16

The Rhapsodes

HOW 1940S

CRITICS CHANGED

AMERICAN FILM

CULTURE

DAVID BORDWELL

THE UNIVERSITY OF CHICAGO PRESS
Chicago and London

DAVID BORDWELL is the Jacques Ledoux Professor of Film Studies Emeritus at the University of Wisconsin–Madison. With Kristin Thompson, he is coauthor of *Film Art: An Introduction* and *Film History: An Introduction* and the blog *Observations on Film Art*, which can be found at http://www.davidbordwell.net/blog.

The University of Chicago Press, Chicago 60637
The University of Chicago Press, Ltd., London
© 2016 by The University of Chicago
All rights reserved. Published 2016.
Printed in the United States of America

25 24 23 22 21 20 19 18 17 16   1 2 3 4 5

ISBN-13: 978-0-226-35217-6 (cloth)
ISBN-13: 978-0-226-35220-6 (paper)
ISBN-13: 978-0-226-35234-3 (e-book)
DOI: 10.7208/chicago/9780226352343.001.0001

LIBRARY OF CONGRESS CATALOGING-IN-PUBLICATION DATA

Bordwell, David, author.
   The Rhapsodes : how 1940s critics changed American film culture / David Bordwell.
      pages ; cm
   Includes bibliographical references and index.
   ISBN 978-0-226-35217-6 (cloth : alk. paper) — ISBN 978-0-226-35220-6 (pbk. : alk. paper) — ISBN 978-0-226-35234-3 (e-book) 1. Film criticism—United States—History—20th century. 2. Film critics—United States. 3. Ferguson, Otis, 1907–1943. 4. Agee, James, 1909–1955. 5. Farber, Manny. 6. Tyler, Parker. I. Title.
      PN1995.B6177 2016
      791.4301—dc23

                                                                        2015023661

♾ This paper meets the requirements of ANSI/NISO Z39.48-1992 (Permanence of Paper).

For Diane and Darlene
Who always liked to read

In anything fit to be called by the name of reading, the process itself should be absorbing and voluptuous; we should gloat over a book, be rapt clean out of ourselves, and rise from the perusal, our mind filled with the busiest, kaleidoscopic dance of images, incapable of sleep or of continuous thought.

ROBERT LOUIS STEVENSON

Contents

Introduction

If you judge by sheer bulk, film criticism is flourishing as never before. Despite signs of a struggling newspaper industry, every major city, from New York and Los Angeles to Detroit and Phoenix, hosts a society of journalist-reviewers. Critics swarm across our screens too—writing for online magazines, chatting in podcasts and YouTube clips, tweeting their instant reactions. The Online Film Critics Society listed over 250 members in 2014. Two aggregators, Rotten Tomatoes and Metacritic, track many of these writers, but hundreds more eager amateurs and would-be professionals fill personal websites with thoughts about movies old and new.

The more visible movie reviewing becomes, though, the less important any one reviewer seems. Although a few elite critics remain powers to be reckoned with, they enjoy far less fame than the mighty figures of the 1960s and 1970s. Andrew Sarris, Pauline Kael, and Roger Ebert became more famous than most of the movies they wrote about, and upon their deaths they were the subjects of more eulogies and memoirs than most departed filmmakers. They survive in cinephile memory as emblems of a time when film criticism ascended into the world of letters.

In earlier decades Vachel Lindsay, H.D., Carl Sandburg, and Graham Greene tried their hand at film pieces, but they had established their fame in other domains. In the 1960s, however, Kael, Sarris, Stanley Kauffmann, and a host of others treated film reviewing as not merely a report on current releases but an occasion for a display of the writer's sensibility. Still others, like Dwight Macdonald, John Simon, and Susan Sontag, wrote about the arts generally, but their fame depended heavily on what they said about movies.

"I read X," people started to say, "not because I care much about current films but because the critic is such a good *writer*, such an interesting *person*." (Bosley Crowther, eternal straw man who wrote for the *Times*, failed the charisma test; besides, he didn't get *Bonnie and Clyde*.) For the new film critics, a film's release became less the object of judgment than the springboard for prose high dives, weekly or monthly or quarterly performances of verbal bravado and quarrelsome risk taking. Film criticism began to host a cult of personality, even an elite branding. Kael and Sarris came to my college campus in 1965, set to "debate" movies' status as an art. Ten years later, Ebert won the first Pulitzer Prize awarded to a film critic.

In all the spite, vanity, teacup tempests, and conceptual confusions of the era, there were some long-lasting critical achievements. These 1960s writers showed that journalistic film criticism could be as idiosyncratic and intimate as the writing of, say, George Bernard Shaw on music and theater. And you could gain fans and fame solely *as* a critic; you wouldn't have to write *Mrs. Warren's Profession*.

If I had to pick one pivot point for the beginning of this new age, I'd choose 16 May 1955. On that day James Agee had a fatal heart attack in a New York taxicab. Two years later *A Death in the Family* was published. Despite being unfinished, the novel won enormous praise and was awarded the Pulitzer Prize. Agee's renewed fame led to the publication in 1958 of *Agee on Film: Reviews and Comments*. The collection revealed that a man of letters who was largely unappreciated by the literary establishment during his lifetime had spent precious creative years, week in and week out, reviewing movies for both a highbrow liberal weekly, the *Nation*, and the mass-market *Time*.

Suddenly people recognized that a magazine column passing judgment on the week's releases could display graceful style and probing thought. *Agee on Film* reprinted a 1944 encomium from W. H. Auden, who called Agee's column "newspaper work of permanent literary value" and "the most remarkable regular event in journalism today." A review of the 1958 collection in the *New York Times* declared that Agee's fierce love for cinema "gave him a deeper insight into the nature of the movie medium, *in esse* and *in posse*, than any other American with the possible exception of Gilbert Seldes." The *Saturday Review* reached higher: "He was the best movie critic this country has ever had."

There's no knowing how many teenagers and twentysomethings read and reread that fat paperback with its blaring red cover. We wolfed it down without knowing most of the movies Agee discussed. We were held, I think, by the rolling lyricism of the sentences, the pawky humor, and the stylistic finish of certain pieces—the three-part essay on *Monsieur Verdoux*, the *Life* piece "Comedy's Greatest Era," the John Huston profile "Undirectable Director." The adolescent fretfulness that put some critics off didn't give us qualms; after all, we were unashamedly reading Hart Crane, Thomas Wolfe, and J. D. Salinger. Some of us probably wished we could some day write this way, and this well.

The timing of the collection proved ideal. The status of film criticism in the 1960s was being boosted by intellectuals' interest in movies. More people were going to college, and some of them were drawn to foreign imports (Bergman, Antonioni, Kurosawa, Godard, Truffaut) and new American cinema (*Dr. Strangelove*, *The Graduate*, *Bonnie and Clyde*, *Easy Rider*). Such unusual movies demanded commentary, even debate. This was the moment that made the movie review or the longish think piece a respectable literary genre.

During the 1940s two of the major British reviewers, James Agate and C. A. Lejeune, had gathered their movie journalism in book form, and even in the United States critics-at-large like Mark Van Doren and John Mason Brown had bundled their film reviews with their literary essays. But Agee was, as James Naremore has pointed out, the most famous American literary figure to review movies at the time. The posthumous anthology of his articles not only enhanced his standing but gave film journalism a new stature. Mass-market periodicals, political magazines, and literary quarterlies (*Kenyon Review*, *Sewanee Review*, *Southern Review*, *Hudson Review*, etc.) decided they needed movie coverage, and a new generation of writers came forward.

It took a little while for book publishers to sense that a market was there, but eventually anthologies formed a genre. *Agee on Film* was the model for Pauline Kael's *I Lost It at the Movies* (1965), which became something of a best seller. Between 1960 and 1973, I count over twenty collections of reviews by Kael and Hollis Alpert, John Simon, Stanley Kauffmann, Raymond Durgnat, Judith Crist, Renata Adler, Dwight Macdonald, Andrew Sarris, Herman G. Weinberg, Graham Greene, Richard Schickel, William S. Pechter, Rex Reed, and Vernon Young. That doesn't include the mixed cinema and literature anthologies signed by Susan Sontag, Penelope Gilliatt, Wilfred Sheed, and others.

The burst of cut-and-paste collections swept two of Agee's contemporaries back into view. Parker Tyler and Manny Farber began their careers in the 1940s, and they hadn't exactly been silent since then. Tyler wrote voluminously throughout the 1950s and 1960s, and he published a collection, *The Three Faces of the Film* (1960), in the wake of the Agee anthology. There followed another gathering, *Sex Psyche Etcetera in the Film* (1969). More important was the 1970 reprinting of Tyler's first two books of criticism: *The Hollywood Hallucination* (1944) and *Magic and Myth of the Mov-*

ies (1947). Tyler's contemporary Manny Farber gathered several pieces, mostly from the 1950s and 1960s, into *Negative Space* (1971).

Probably neither Tyler nor Farber would have returned to fame without the canonization of Agee. Their near contemporary Otis Ferguson had been killed in the war, but the film-book boom revived his reputation as well, with his collected reviews appearing in 1971. Agee's death revealed that he was part of a cadre who had, to little notice at the time, powerfully raised the quality of popular film commentary. These four writers made criticism more than a vehicle for ephemeral observations and displays of taste: it became a serious (though often sprightly) inquiry into how Hollywood movies worked.

The Rhapsodes is an essayistic examination of the critical practice of Ferguson, Agee, Farber, and Tyler: the most significant American film critics of the 1940s. Their work, deliberately different from that of their peers in other arts, tried to capture—sometimes analytically, sometimes poetically—what they found moving, artful, or disappointing in American cinema. Largely ignored by official culture, they came to wider recognition decades later, after film criticism emerged as a legitimate area of arts journalism. The celebrity critics of the 1960s, as well as the top critics of today and the squadrons of bloggers, owe a great deal to these four men. They laid the foundations for the 1960s renaissance.

They wrote at a crucial moment in film history. They tracked the golden age of Hollywood, that period from the mid-1930s to the early 1950s in which the Hollywood system was, quite simply, The Movies. When Ferguson started, the studios had just mastered talkies, and he was fascinated by how a new tradition of visual storytelling had absorbed lifelike dialogue and a Depression-era concern with everyday life. Agee and Farber chronicled the studios' war effort, while assessing the new realism of combat and urban melodrama. Agee proved sympathetic to the home front drama and comedy, while Farber bore witness to the brutal action pictures the French would label *film noir*. At the same time, Hollywood began seriously, or rather unseriously, incorporating dreams, psychoanalysis, and myth into its tales, and Tyler was fully up to the challenge. Taken together, these critics offer us Hollywood without nostalgia, as a sprawling phenomenon trying to innovate, to turn a buck, and to figure itself out.

It isn't just history that's at stake: these 1940s writers still have a lot to teach us. They remain far more provocative and penetrating than nearly anyone writing film criticism today. They are also fine artists in prose.

If a worthy critic must be an exceptional writer, my four critics meet the standard. They created their distinctive idioms out of the turbulent, knockabout language of a country that came up with *snafu* and *hokum* and *hen fruit* and *the Ameche* (for the telephone, because Don Ameche invented it, as Sugarpuss O'Shea explains in *Ball of Fire*, 1941). The critics' lingo wasn't merely showing off. They sought to change a situation expressed concisely by Ferguson: "Film criticism is obediently dull and uninformative, and surely unworthy of so lively and immanent a subject."

Ferguson, who wrote for the *New Republic* from 1934 to 1942, is a natural starting point for our story. While reviewing the weekly releases, he laid out some terms for appreciating Hollywood sound cinema as a whole. The well-wrought movie, he thought, would be "smooth, fast-moving, effortless." It would display an honest, unshowy naturalism about how people behave—particularly how they do their work. It would integrate revealing details and moments of emotional impact into an arc of clean, cogent action, both physical and dramatic.

Ferguson left film reviewing in 1942 for the Merchant Marine and died early in World War II. Three critics who had begun writing around 1940 continued on his way, each in idiosyncratic fashion. Agee, Farber, and Tyler wrote criticism that was pungent, slangy, creatively ungrammatical. They accepted the advantages of minor genres and pushed very hard against highbrow tastes. They had an eye for technique as it might work in privileged moments to convey character or the taste of reality. And they freshened up the familiar faults-and-beauties rhetoric of reviewing with paradox (Farber), a search for exactitude of judgment (Agee), and a calm willingness to go beyond the bounds of reason (Tyler).

My first chapter calls the four of them the Rhapsodes, by analogy with the ancient reciters of verse who, inspired by the gods, became carried away. The tag aims to emphasize the exuberance of their vernacular prose. Of course they weren't really carried away: they were wholly in charge. They were seeking to differentiate themselves as personalities while conveying something of the punch and swing of the movies themselves. Beyond the appeal of their writing, they reveal to us the promise and problems of American film culture in the 1940s. Whether praising or denouncing the weekly releases, what did these smart people think film had been, was, could be? What were the artistic prospects of Hollywood cinema?

As both thinkers and prose artists, they broke with the urbane gatekeepers of their day as well as with the writers who populated the intellectual journals. Those journals were glumly starting to report a disenchantment with Stalinism and a realization that the Soviet Union would not be the land of avant-garde art. The best hope for art now was a culture centered on high modernism and its heirs. Accordingly, for the serious elite, Hollywood films were the most threatening face of mass culture. Manufactured in bulk and jammed down the throats of the unwary multitudes, movies were a betrayal of art—a turning away from both the authenticity of folk art and the revolutionary force of the avant-garde. The result was, inevitably, that movies could only be kitsch.

I suggest in the second chapter that the Rhapsodes detoured skillfully around the arguments about mass culture. They found new ways of talking about popular art. At this period, new methods of "close reading" had emerged in literary studies, musicology, and art history. Obviously film critics couldn't examine their "texts" as minutely as critics of other media could; there was no home video, and no accessible way to study current releases on viewing machines. Still, within the constraints of the time, these critics managed to subject films to scrutiny. And their probing of particular shots and scenes was a powerful counter to the vague denunciations of the *Partisan Review* crowd.

The first barrier was recognizing film as a valid popular art. Already some of Hollywood's admirers put story first and recognized that the liveliest film was often the unpretentious comedy or melodrama. Prestige pictures, especially literary adaptations, were no guarantee of vitality. What makes this vitality possible, Ferguson maintained, is a discreet technique. "The very reason you don't see it is its own justification: you are not conscious of camera or effects, for the little bit flickers past in the final version and you are conscious only that a story is starting as you follow. Only!"

Although the mechanics might be invisible to the audience, Ferguson thought critics should be more curious. Here he parted company with most of his peers. A critic, he insisted, should not be a dilettante. The critic should possess "a constant and humble passion to know everything of what is being done and how everything is being done." As a jazz critic, he benefited from knowing the tricks of that trade, and late in his career he visited Hollywood to watch filmmakers like William Wyler and Fritz Lang at work. Firsthand observation is one way to appreciate honest craft: "The camera way is the hard way." Focusing on the planning and labor of production led him to an early form of close reading, as I'll try to show in chapter 3.

Ferguson's peers found other detours. Agee was since his youth a film fan who wrote imaginary screenplays flaunting sheer technique. These practice pieces sensitized him to the possibilities of filmic creation. Farber, trained as a painter, brought a concern with fastidious craft, pictorial design, and emotional expressivity to his thinking about films. Parker Tyler, a Surrealist poet, had an eye for evanescent detail that would allow him to expand associatively from an image or story premise to some surprising implications.

Agee, I argue in the fourth chapter, possessed a Romantic sensibility. Both outward-looking and introspective, he hoped for poetic revelations from cinema; he also dramatized, in his probing hesitations, the very difficulty of finding those flashes of illumination. His fiction and reportage sought "the illusion of embodiment" and the piercing moment of emotion, both of which cinema could sometimes provide. His short reviews in the *Nation* throughout the 1940s often only hinted at these qualities, but his longer pieces developed the possibilities further. He offered a New Critical interpretation of Charles Chaplin's *Monsieur Verdoux* and an essay discussing the visual strategies of John Huston.

Agee's contemporary and sometime rival Manny Farber has become famous as the most pictorially sensitive critic of the time, one who brought his awareness of modernist painting to bear on movies. But this standard view needs nuance, or so I argue in the fifth chapter. For one thing, modern painting in the approved sense of the 1940s—chiefly, abstract painting as praised by Clement Greenberg—didn't get full backing in Farber's art reviews. I try to show that Farber was receptive to all manner of representational art besides abstraction. More important, he was in a rather old-fashioned way committed to emotional expression. Contra Greenberg, Farber also welcomed popular graphic art, comic strips included.

By the time he came to movies, Farber was able to focus more acutely on visual detail than Agee did. Over a few years of reviewing for the *New Republic* (1942–46), he moved toward vivid evocations of space in cinema. Yet these, I argue, didn't reflect the ideology of modernist painting. Farber agreed with Ferguson that Hollywood was committed to smooth storytelling. He thus believed that film was an appropriate home for the "illusionism" and "illustration" that the Greenberg school condemned.

It was only later that Farber saw Hollywood as converging with modern painting, and he found that trend objectionable. In 1950 he wrote, "Directors, by flattening the screen, discarding framing and centered action, and looming the importance of actors—have made the movie come out and hit the audience with almost personal savagery." Shadowboxing with Agee, Farber objected to John Huston's crowded, self-consciously composed frames. Throughout this period, Farber adhered to Ferguson's aesthetic of crisp, lean storytelling that didn't call attention to itself.

Parker Tyler didn't worry so much about storytelling, smooth or otherwise. Instead, in the Surrealist tradition of "irrational enlargement" of moments in the films he saw, his books *The Hollywood Hallucination* (1944) and *Magic and Myth of the Movies* (1947) looked for cracks in the polished surface of Hollywood narration. Chopping plots to bits, he sought mythic and Freudian reverberations in the most mundane pictures. And as a gay man he had no hesitation about undermining the gender implications of everything he saw.

Serious thinkers called Hollywood a dream factory, but Tyler went further. He redreamed what was on the screen. He celebrated the "baroque energy and protean symbolism" of stars (really, charade performers), stories (with their suggestive imagery and charmingly conventional closure), and special effects (summoning the wayward appeals of primitive magic). Chapter 6 shows how Tyler, seeking scandalous entertainment value in Hollywood, was driven to scrutinize the films with a sensitivity comparable to Agee's and Farber's. Working at book length, he could develop his claims more fully than a reviewer could, on a scale appropriate to the Hollywood Hallucination itself. At the same time, the *sprezzatura* of his critical performance made him no less a conjurer with the American language than his contemporaries.

The final chapter offers some reflections on the legacy of my critical quartet. Ferguson and Agee didn't live to see the film generation of the 1960s or the rise of celebrity criticism. But Farber and Tyler, in characteristic ways, participated in the new film culture. At the same time, each kept alive certain major aspects of his youth—Farber in his celebration of 1940s action films, Tyler in asserting the continuing relevance of the poetic avant-garde.

More generally, by rereading these creative critics we can see the emergence of conceptions of American cinema that remain with us. In the 1940s, many intellectuals gave earlier generations' mistrust of popular culture a new legitimacy through a harsh denunciation of "mass culture." These writers, after the shock of Stalinism and the commercialization of American art and literature, clung to high modernism. They bewailed Hollywood as the essence of lowbrow culture (bad) and middlebrow culture (worse). Another wing of intellectuals, granting the brow debates some legitimacy, sought to interpret Hollywood as the unconscious mirror of American ideals, anxieties, and moods.

Today the battle for high-low-middlebrow culture is over. It may have ended as early as the 1950s, when Harold Rosenberg complained, "That kitsch and life are grown together into one monstrous limb may very well be at the bottom of the new delusion that the secrets of existence can now be read on the movie screen." But the other intellectual flanking maneuver of the forties, that of reading popular films as reflecting the zeitgeist, is still flourishing. Look no further than your favorite newspaper or movie website.

My critics seldom argued with these positions explicitly. Practical aesthetes, they got on with the business of understanding Hollywood movies as an art form. Ferguson provided a rationale for Hollywood's own artistic ideals of narrative clarity, emotional engagement, and the pleasure of familiar tales well told. Agee agreed but went further, suggesting that occasionally Hollywood could capture something deeper than the home truths prized by Ferguson: a transporting glimpse of human possibility. For Farber, by contrast, the best films' sharp and emotionally expressive storytelling was enhanced by the sort of pictorial intelligence that adherents of abstract painting had rejected. Tyler proposed another way to understand Hollywood: as a super-art that, for all its surface sheen and propulsive drama, enjoyed creating dislocations. The play, he asserted against Ferguson, was not the thing. In trying to blend story, star, genre, spectacle, and enticing subjects and themes, the Hollywood movie wound up something of a mess—a game of artifice that could turn poignant or sinister.

These views still bear fruit in our time. The Ferguson-Agee-Farber view that mass-market cinema has created a powerful artistic tradition is virtually the founding gesture of both mass-market film criticism and academic film studies. Tyler's reading of the Hollywood Hallucination for pleasure and *dépaysement* has found its heirs in our academics who probe movies for mythical maneuvers and psychoanalytic dynamics. Meanwhile, fans of Bad Movies, Guilty Pleasures, and various kinds of Camp carry on Tyler's effort to quarry fugitive moments that will yield a disconcerting buzz.

The book closes by situating the homegrown critical sensibility of these writers in relation to what emerged in Paris over the same years. French cinephilia, typified by the brilliance of André Bazin, helped create contemporary film criticism, both popular and academic. Part of my job is to show that the Rhapsodes can be no less inspiring, if only we pay attention.

1 *The Rhapsodes*

In February 1942, Otis Ferguson speculated that a new generation of critics could revitalize popular thinking about film.

> More people go to good and bad movies than read good and bad books, and surely the top layer of this vast audience is as discriminating of taste and exacting of standards as the top layer of the reading public. . . . There are plenty of young people growing up to whom the films are so natural that they do not have to play the snob about them. Bright people too, who can tell you what makes a screen story tick.

By the time "The Case of the Critics" appeared in the *New Republic*, Ferguson had shipped out for war. He left behind more than admonitions. From his first reviews of 1934, he had set out some premises for a defense of the Hollywood movie. His parting essay was pessimistic, but it held out the possibility that a younger critic could keep testing these premises within the changing situation of current filmmaking. What progress had been made? Had current filmmakers forgotten the achievements of mature talking pictures? And how did you not play the snob?

Three critics in effect took up Ferguson's call. In 1942 James Agee was thirty-three and Manny Farber was twenty-six. Their youth, I think, made them plucky enough to think boldly about commercial cinema in America. Tyler was thirty-eight, but hardly a sober citizen; he hadn't lost the impertinence that made him call himself, during his earliest days in Manhattan, the Beautiful Poet Parker Tyler. He too would try rethinking Hollywood.

Neither highbrow nor lowbrow nor middlebrow, neither pure journalists nor Algonquin intellectuals, these four created a daredevil criticism that was audacious and dazzling. They stayed largely outside the critical establishment. In an era when most young arts journalists wanted to be either Edmund Wilson or Alexander Woollcott, they insisted on being themselves.

Each of the quartet displayed a fine intelligence trained in the high arts, particularly modernist trends. Yet each bypassed the current debates on mass culture and plunged directly into the stuff itself, unashamed. Each man urged his readers to see things in movies that more overtly serious intellectuals missed. Each cultivated a writing style that evoked a sharply etched personality. And each strategically lapsed into rhapsodic, occasionally nutty outbursts unlike anything on offer from their staid contemporaries.

It took only a few years for Ferguson's unsnobbish successors to become entrenched in magazines both little and big. Tyler, who produced a 1940 account of *Rebecca* and *Blondie on a Budget* for the Surrealist *View*, kept writing about film for coterie journals and published three books in the decade. In late 1942 Agee wrote his first film reviews for the *Nation* and *Time*. In 1942 Farber started covering film for the *New Republic*, taking up Ferguson's column. Agee gave up film criticism at the end of the 1940s, but Farber and Tyler kept publishing into the 1970s.

Ferguson, Agee, and Farber were weekly journalists, while Tyler practiced belles lettres in the pages of art journals and little magazines. Ferguson brought to serious film criticism the tang of Depression newshawk jauntiness. Every paragraph became a freewheeling adventure in slang, mixed metaphors, and yoyo syntax. Agee and Farber opened that vein further and mined it for more glittering ore. Parker Tyler went his own way, offering what he called later "the straight face of high camp" and wrote with "tongue stiff in cheek."

All were polymaths, bringing experiences of other arts to bear on the cinema. Over nine years at the *New Republic* Ferguson reviewed books as well as movies, at the same time becoming one of the day's best writers on jazz. Agee was a poet, novelist, screenwriter, book reviewer, journalist, and author of one of the landmark books of the 1940s, *Let Us Now Praise Famous Men*. Manny Farber, while writing reviews and working as a carpenter, pursued a career as a painter. Tyler wrote poetry, a scandalous experimental novel about gay life, and essays and books on the fine arts.

At the same time, all were cinephiles. They knew the standard story of film history, handily traced in Paul Rotha's *The Film Till Now* (1930) and Lewis Jacobs's *Rise of the American Film* (1939). Their canon was, by today's standards, very cramped. It consisted mostly of Museum of Modern Art touchstones and Manhattan revival staples: D. W. Griffith (for some shorts and *The Birth of a Nation*), the silent clowns (Chaplin above all), *Caligari, The Battleship Potemkin* (sometimes *Earth*), and René Clair's *The Italian Straw Hat* and his early sound pictures. Yet the critics agreed that however great the classics remained, and however terrible contemporary Hollywood could be, there were extraordinary things to be found in new releases.

Beauty, in Flashes

What sorts of things? Beautiful things. These critics seem to me aesthetes pursuing modern beauty from various angles. Ferguson sought out a proletarian vigor, a clean, sharp art that carried the breath of ordinary living. Agee was a Romantic, Farber an eclectic modernist. Tyler was an avant-garde dandy in the Wilde-Cocteau tradition. Their attitudes had been established in the sacred precincts of literature and painting but hadn't made their way to the criticism of mass entertainment.

Moreover, the four critics understood that movies stretched the very standards and premises of high art. Most intellectuals had thought you couldn't talk about a Cary Grant movie as an artwork. Ferguson and company understood that you could, if you favored criteria like liveliness, poignancy, force, and arresting detail. Most intellectuals couldn't recognize art in mass-market movies because Hollywood had redefined what artistry was. At moments Hollywood had taken creativity *beyond* art, into a realm that Tyler called hallucination.

The beauty these four disclosed was often merely glimpsed. Ferguson cared more than the others about a movie's unity, but all of them realized that in the popular media, parts sometimes outranked wholes. Most movies lacked the formal rigor of classic art. Instead of finding this worrisome, these writers found it exhilarating. Each one was alert to momentary diversions, odd spots, places where something unpredictable seemed to leak in around the cracks.

The idea that Hollywood movies sometimes yielded fugitive moments of truth wasn't uncommon in the period. Barbara Deming, looking for symptoms of American malaise, suggested that actors occasionally "scuffed in" a tangible reality of behavior that couldn't be manufactured, and Dwight Macdonald conceded that the system sometimes turned out films with moments of vitality. Vitality was precious to my four essayists too, but they probed further. They suggested that a good part of the artistry, or at least the fascination, of popular movies lies exactly in those details or plot turns or performance bits or throwaway compositions.

The vagrant items might enrich the action or detour it. Sometimes directors and actors designed the casual bits to yield flashes of diversion or glimpses of real life.

> [Hitchcock] loads his set with [details] without loading down his action; and because everything and everybody aren't direct accessories to the plot, so many mechanical aids, you get the effect of life, which also has its dogs and casual passers-by who are real without having anything to do with any plot you know about. (Ferguson on *Foreign Correspondent*)

> These actors produce some light, whimsical effects which are generally minor as far as making the plot any more significant, but they are the most intriguing parts of the film and were generally intended by the director. (Farber on *The Mask of Dimitrios*)

> [The film includes] purely "meaningless" bits—such as a shot in which Ernie Pyle (Burgess Meredith) sits by the road while some soldiers straggle past—which have as great meaning as anything could have, being as immediate and as unlimited by thought or prejudice as what the eye might see on the spot, in a casual glance. (Agee on *The Story of G.I. Joe*)

At other times, the surprising bits seemed to come with the territory—the story, the conditions of stardom, or simply the accidents of location filming. For Tyler, the blooming pleasures were at their best when inadvertent.

> The voice [is] an independent actor, an element that, as with all Hollywood components, refuses to be completely absorbed into the artistic mesh and creates a little theater of its own.

He thought that most films lurched from moment to striking moment, leaving piquant dissonances behind. "Crevices," he called them.

These critics accordingly recast one of the conventions of film reviewing: the rhetoric of faults and beauties. *This moment is rather nice, but that one falls flat. . . . The dullness of the affair is alleviated by a flash of comedy from a young woman we hope to see again. . . . Brilliant as it is, the film suffers from a certain stiffness. . . .* Unless you're writing a hatchet job, you must dose your praise with some vinegar, and you must dilute your severity with a few compliments.

Our four critics turn faults-and-beauties criticism to fresh purposes. Agee uses it to whip himself into loops of indecision. Writing up *Till the Clouds Roll By*, he notes that the story is feeble but the players are "nice people" and the songs are by Jerome Kern. Phrase by phrase he gives, then takes away, then gives again.

> If, as I do, you like a good deal of his graceful, nacreous music, the picture is pleasantly, if rather stupefyingly, worth all the bother. The songs are nearly all sung with care and affection, though not one that I have heard before is done here quite as well as I have heard it elsewhere.

Farber likewise crosscuts his praise and blame, but in a sardonic vein. On the "well-played and punchy" *Home of the Brave*, which he declares "a clattering, virile movie with deeply affecting moments," we also get this:

> The script is so basically theatrical that it has to be acted almost entirely from seated or reclining positions, but the director works more variations on those two positions than can be found in a Turkish bath. The actors talk as though they were trying to drill the words into one another's skulls; this savage portentousness not only forces your interest but is alarming in that the soldiers are usually surrounded by Japs and every word can obviously be heard in Tokyo.

If Agee is Hamlet, Farber plays Hotspur. Ferguson works the plus-and-minus game for gags.

> I count it a prize, though not doubting it has some awful things wrong. I lost track. I would like to be a good critic and keep a severe check on whether Values are realized and all, but I kept falling out of my seat, and so the best I can say about *Sing and Like It* is, It's probably a lousy picture but you fall out of your seat.

Tyler treats faults and beauties as almost interchangeable. Since the pleasure of thinking about Hollywood movies consists partly in quickening their clichés with jolts of your imagination, the faults become valuable points of interest and, perversely, blossom into virtues. Such is the picture of Dorian Gray in Albert Lewin's film. Both Agee and Farber complained that they wanted to see the painting deteriorate in stages, but Tyler finds the abrupt revelation of the picture in its horrific final stage, dialed up by shrieking Technicolor, as morbidly appealing as a flowering nightshade.

> It is proof of Hollywood's commendably alert, albeit limited imagination. . . . Although art is implicitly offended, one cannot help reacting with a certain thrill. It is the way one usually reacts to zombies and werewolves from the jungles adjacent to Sunset Boulevard. Ivan Le Loraine Albright has given us in his portrait of Dorian the wicked, a compelling version of the American moral jungle from which fundamentally all famous creeps must be said to crepitate.

Even flagrant errors of taste, Tyler suggests, can create teasing crevices to be probed by the critic's imagination.

Speaking in Tongues

The standard images have endured. Ferguson gives out with the reporter's snappy patter, Agee is the sensitive and sentimental humanist, Farber the poolroom wiseacre who reads *Art News*, Tyler the hyperintellectual dilettante who does a couch job on the movies. But this lineup does them a discredit. Basically, all four function as performers.

Writing about movies allows them to do the police in different voices, to spread out American idioms like a magician fanning a fistful of cards. The staccato prose carries us through mixed metaphors, dropped conjunctions, and ricocheting associations. Here is Otis Ferguson on Stokowski conducting *Fantasia*:

> As a background and continuum for this there is the noise and motion of an orchestra assembling and tuning up, than which there is nothing more fascinating, nothing more exciting with promise in the world. But over and above this, on some kind of promontory and silhouetted in awful color is Dr. Leopold in a claw-hammer coat, leading with expression that only falls short of balancing a seal on its nose an orchestra which made that part of the soundtrack yesterday in shirtsleeves and is at the moment out for a cigarette. I rarely bray aloud in the theatre, as this is rude and also may get you into an argument with men who have muscles in their arms, but when Dr. L yearned out over the strings to the left of him in a passage for horns (which are in the center when

they're there at all) and the bedazzlement of color yearned sympathetically from baby-blue to baby-something-else, I released a short one.

Mind you, Ferguson adores Disney, and *Fantasia* in particular. Very soon after the passage quoted, he says this of the film:

Dull as it is toward the end, ridiculous as it is in the bend of the knee before Art, and taking one thing with another, it is one of the strange and beautiful things that have happened in the world.

Few other writers would give us that first "and." We would expect "*but* taking one thing with another, it is . . ." This twist of phrase, anticipated by the earlier thumping coda ("I released a short one"), sets the keynote for the criticism of Agee, Farber, and Tyler. Ferguson jiggled and snapped a sentence like a lariat. He showed by example that criticism could be a fine unsnobbish show, a prose cabaret.

In his wake, Agee, Tyler, and Farber become pop culture Rhapsodes, writing in a divine frenzy. These bards aren't kissed by the gods, though. They're carried away by having found a subject—movies—that triggers a controlled ecstasy. The result is usually comic, sometimes dramatic, often sensuously arousing. An orgy of words, after all, is still an orgy.

Farber, of course, is celebrated for his baroque firepower, fueled by paradox and hyperbole. The sentences seem to veer out of control before ending with a wisecrack that's sometimes a capper and sometimes just weird.

The movie, "The Postman Always Rings Twice," is almost too terrible to walk out of. . . . The wife spends her time in what should be a jungle washing the several thousand stunning play suits she wears to wait on tables, going for moonlight swims, dancing stylish rumbas with the hobo. I think the best bobby-sox touches are the white turban that Cora wears to wash dishes, the love scenes which show Cora in a yum-yum pose and outfit, looking like a frozen popsicle, with Frank ogling her at six paces—and probably the director, in the background, swooning over a hamburger.

Where to start? "Too terrible to walk out of" is already something to chew on, suggesting that genuine awfulness can be enjoyed, but the extra "almost" creates a mental jujitsu throw. Should we walk out or not? And why should the gas station be a jungle? The hyperbolic description of Cora's wardrobe is discreetly qualified by that "several," which makes sure we don't think that she has only a *few* thousand playsuits. Comparing Cora to a popsicle is already bold enough, but most editors would cut "frozen" as redundant; yet it helps reinforce her ice queen aloofness. Then there's the absurd specification of Frank's distance as "six paces," no more nor less, as if the critic had stepped it out on the sound stage. (The phrase also evokes a marksman on the target range or a duelist sizing up an opponent.) As for director Tay Garnett swooning not over Lana Turner but over a hamburger, your guess is as good as mine.

Want something more refined but no less gaga? Here is Tyler, in one of my favorite passages of American film criticism, on Lauren Bacall in *To Have and Have Not.*

> I was still transfixed by the conundrum of her voice, almost without inflection, low and lazily paced, with a pleasant burr of the Dietrich sort but not classifiable as to its true sources. . . . That she approached Hollywood with a certain Machiavellianism, I think, is shown by the mild Mephistophelian peaks of her eyebrows. Yet all of us are human; the most sensational military plans, even if the army wins, sometimes go kerflooey. Miss Bacall had evidently intended her voice to give notice that she was a Garbo to the gizzard, hard to get, and not going to let Humphrey triumph at the first shot.

I don't think *Mephistophelian* has ever been juxtaposed with *kerflooey* so effectively.

Agee, taken by many today as a gentle soul who leaned too much on his lyrical gifts, proves ready to spin us into orbit in reviewing the Warners cartoon *Rhapsody Rabbit*. Bugs Bunny as a concert pianist gives "a cut but definitive performance" of a Liszt *Hungarian Rhapsody*.

> The best part of it goes two ways: one, very observant parody of concert-pianistic affectations, elegantly thought out and synchronized; the other, brutality keyed into the spirit of the music to reach greater subtlety than I have ever seen brutality reach before. I could hardly illustrate without musical quotation; but there is a passage in which the music goes up with an arrogant wrenching of

1.1 *Rhapsody Rabbit* (1946).

slammed chords—Ronk, *Ronk*, RONK (G-B-E)—then prisses down-
ward on a broken scale—which Bugs takes (a) with all four feet,
charging madly, scowling like a rockinghorse late for a date at stud,
(b) friskily tiptoe, proudly smirking, like a dog toe-dancing through
his own misdemeanor or the return of an I-Was-There journalist, a
man above fear or favor who knows precisely which sleeping dogs
to lie about. It killed me; and when they had the wonderful brass to
repeat it exactly, a few bars later, I knew what killed really meant.

Grant the juxtaposition, common to all these critics, of high and low
speech (*affectations* and *misdemeanor* versus *prisses* and *killed me*). And
grant that this new demotic spares no time for niceties like quotation
marks indicating that you're referring to a word ("I knew what killed
really meant"). The longer you look at this passage, the more outrageous
it gets. A rocking horse put out to stud? Presumably that's Bugs's lusty
prancing. But a dog's "misdemeanor"—pissing on the carpet? And Fido
with a proud smirk? How did the on-the-spot journalist get in here? And
was the travesty of the "sleeping dogs lie" cliché suggested by association
with the balletic, bladder-emptied dog? Agee usually wrote more linear
sentences, trembling and hesitant though they could be. On occasions

like this, though, he could also unleash some benign madness. But of course the craftsman never left the controls: all the parallel clauses are set into balance by stately semicolons.

At times you have to wonder if there wasn't a sort of prose arms race among the three young ones, each pushing beyond Ferguson to convey the elusive rush of the movie under their eyes. In any event, what the Rhapsodes accomplished in fifteen years remains flat-out astonishing. They made American English sing at a fresh pace and pitch. They made writing about film exuberant and important. They raised arts criticism to a level of frenzied acuity it had seldom enjoyed. They helped create, after some delay, the modern institution of American movie criticism, with all its virtues and excesses. In the process, they forged some original ways of thinking about Hollywood cinema.

2 *A Newer Criticism*

The 1940s were a golden age of American arts journalism. Apart from Edmund Wilson, who had been at it since the 1920s, Randall Jarrell, Karl Shapiro, W. H. Auden, and Mary McCarthy were offering their thoughts on literature to a broad public. Professional critics included Lionel Trilling, Jacques Barzun, Irving Howe, and Leslie Fiedler. Clement Greenberg reviewed art for the *Nation*, and Harold Rosenberg did the same for *Art News*. Virgil Thomson wrote weekly music reviews for the *New York Herald Tribune*.

One wing of this East Coast cadre, coming up in the antic twenties and the cynical-idealistic thirties, put on display scathing wit and sibylline prose. Pound and Hemingway, Joyce and Eliot were already comfortably under their belts, and their models didn't come from the *New York Times* or the *Saturday Review of Literature*. Thomson wrote after a concert, "Both theatrical experience and poor eyesight are probably responsible for the Toscanini style." Mary McCarthy skewered Cocteau's play *The Eagle Has Two Heads*:

> Grandiloquent and lurid in the old-fashioned royalist mode, this story of a poet and a queen suggests that the attic of Cocteau's mind was never as smart as the downstairs: a schoolgirl was there all along reading romances and trying on costumes.

This waspish, refined intelligence held the arts to high standards. Apart from Barzun's open admiration for detective stories, almost nobody paid attention to mass culture. Indeed, most intellectuals were agreed that it was dangerous.

This wing of the New York intellectuals—composed of gays, Greenwich Village Bohemians, immigrant-family Jews and Irish denied access to Ivy League colleges, and left-leaning traitors to the upper class—was firmly on the side of modernism and everything else that made the old guard, the WASPs with three names like Henry Seidel Canby and

Mark Van Doren, nervous. But most still had enough of the genteel tradition in them to treat great art with respectful solemnity. The byword of *Partisan Review*, the principal platform of the artistic left, was seriousness.

Enter Otis Ferguson, James Agee, Manny Farber, and Parker Tyler. They wrote criticism with a zany gusto that nobody else imagined possible. They didn't telegraph their punch lines; sometimes you couldn't be sure there was a punch line, and sometimes there were too many. As for popular culture, they seemed, with reservations, to like it a lot. They enjoyed being unserious, which only lent greater oomph to the moments when gravity was demanded.

Neither Dead nor Red

In spite of all these defects you feel in the Soviet Union that you are at the moral top of the world where the light really never goes out.

EDMUND WILSON, 1935

In the 1940s, every intellectual was expected to answer two questions. *What do you think of Communism? What do you think of popular culture?*

The Depression had convinced many writers and artists that only a version of left-wing politics could overcome the crisis induced by capitalism. The rise of Fascist parties had led to right-wing dictatorships. To many intellectuals the Soviet Union seemed the best alternative, especially since its apologists assured the world that it was a democracy. But Stalin's sweeping purge of 1934–38, highlighted by the murderous charade of the Moscow trials, made many lose faith. Soon came the 1939 nonaggression treaty between Russia and Germany, a sign that Stalin was ready to compromise with Nazism.

Dimming faith in the USSR didn't automatically wipe out socialist ambitions. Apart from the Communists, who followed the Moscow line, America played host to a daunting array of left parties: Social Democrats, Socialists, Trotskyists, the Socialist Workers Party, the Socialist Labor Party, and factions within those. Fine-grained differences in doctrine led to constant quarreling. Some intellectuals adhered to one line or another, but many hopped around or simply participated casually, without worrying about ideological consistency, and agreed to donate money or attend meetings or write an article.

When the United States entered World War II in 1941, many intellectuals saw it as a necessary step in destroying Fascism. Now that Russia was an American ally they often tamped down their reservations about

Stalin's regime. At the war's end, however, politicized intellectuals began to believe that Communism was not the path forward. Business and labor had cooperated to defeat German and Japanese imperialism. Despite Marx's predictions, capitalism had lifted the living standards of millions of people. The citizens of the United States were comfortable as never before. American democracy, while imperfect, was still the best chance for mass participation in governance.

Smaller-scale reforms would always be needed, not least the recognition of equality for African Americans, and some form of democratic socialism might still be achieved. But on the whole, the American way of life seemed the best hope for the future. "The chief cultural phenomenon of the decade," noted the poet John Berryman, "has probably been the intellectuals' desertion of Marxism." By 1952, *Partisan Review* declared that democracy was "not merely a capitalist myth but a reality which must be defended against Russian totalitarianism."

Defending American democracy, however, didn't include defending its popular culture.

Mass Art as Mass Delusion

There has been no lack of critics who have proclaimed the uplifting or degrading qualities of the movies without having noticed anything whatever of what was going on in them.

MARSHALL MCLUHAN, 1947

Today, when every intellectual finds something to like in the entertainment industry, it's hard to imagine the climate seventy years ago. Then there was a wide debate about whether mass media were simply machines of social control. From Communists to anti-Communists, the intelligentsia was largely united in the belief that "mass culture" was at best a bland solace and at worst a cruel manipulator of an unhappy populace. Many very smart people considered Bob Hope movies, the *Li'l Abner* comic strip, "Smoke Gets in Your Eyes," and Raymond Chandler novels to be signs of a society sinking into comfortable degradation.

Already during the 1930s, left intellectuals had worried that mainstream American entertainment was corrupt. Not only was the working class victimized by its rulers, it was fed junk. The most influential articulation of this view was probably Clement Greenberg's 1939 essay "Avant-Garde and Kitsch." According to Greenberg, the great age of modern art, from the 1910s to the early 1930s, had showed the power of self-conscious formal experiment. Cubist painting, the novels of Joyce and Gide, the poetry of Eliot—all had challenged the audience to expand its horizons. But to this avant-garde there was counterposed a rear guard, a debased and easy art that produced "unreflective enjoyment." Greenberg didn't exempt the Soviet Union from his complaint: Stalin's Socialist Realism had created its own version of kitsch, in the cinema no less than in other arts.

Greenberg's line of attack was pursued by many others, notably Dwight Macdonald in his 1943 essay "A Theory of 'Popular Culture.'" The common complaint was that now high art was more threatened than ever before by the rising tide of kitsch. For many intellectuals it wasn't just that popular music, comic books, movies, and pulp romances were bad art. They were bad in a dehumanizing way, turning people into more or less mindless consumers of a collective daydream. Mass culture, as it was usually called, was a threat to intellectual diversity and political progress. Conservatives and newly anti-Communist liberals turned their firepower on Hollywood, Tin Pan Alley, Broadway, and the magazines and paperbacks filling the racks at the corner drugstore. For many, political criticism became cultural criticism, with a strongly moralistic tint.

How best to understand the rising tide of mass culture? Some writers, following Greenberg's strategy, counterpointed it to the achievements of the avant-garde. Others drew on psychoanalysis, which was becoming more prominent in American life. Soon writers were claiming that a whole society had a superego and repressed impulses, and that the nation's seething inner life was reflected in popular culture.

Social scientists began commenting as well. Anthropologists turned their observational technique on American culture, and sociologists sought to use media to understand the group dynamics of wartime and postwar society. Other academics, brandishing the tools of what was emerging as "mass communication research," tried to sample and measure the collective delusions promoted on the radio or the movie screen. Émigrés associated with the Frankfurt School merged these strategies with large doses of post-Hegelian philosophy. Adorno and Horkheimer's *Dialectic of Enlightenment* (1944) proposed that American capitalism had turned audiences into chortling morons.

Stuck in the Middle with Middlebrow

Several of these writers had decided by the mid-1940s that Greenberg's straightforward opposition avant-garde/kitsch was too broad. A four-quadrant model seemed more adequate for mapping American culture.

There was folk art, a genuine and spontaneous product of the people. Amish furniture, Appalachian folk songs, and African American spirituals were examples. Some observers included jazz and the blues as well. Folk artists went about their business unbothered by other trends. Another quadrant belonged to highbrow art, exemplified by the modernist avant-garde, past (Joyce, Eliot, Woolf, Stravinsky, Picasso, et al.) and present (perhaps best exemplified in Abstract Expressionist painting). There was lowbrow art, the anonymous products of the culture industry—radio shows, mystery and romance fiction, pop music, and most movies. And there was something called middlebrow art. The term had become fairly common in the 1930s, and 1940s commentators spent a good deal of time trying to figure out what it described.

Certainly it involved class. If high art was consumed by the Bohemians—other artists, museum curators and concert performers, young rebels, and above all college professors and students—middlebrow art was aimed at the middle classes, the professional people who aspired to join the sophisticated crowd. The middlebrows put Renoir reproductions on their walls, Tchaikovsky symphonies on their turntables, and leather-bound, unread editions of Shakespeare's sonnets on their coffee tables alongside *Harper's* or the *Atlantic Monthly*.

Most critics agreed that the middlebrow impulse poached on other realms. There was pseudofolk middlebrow art like WPA murals, *Carmen Jones*, and Gershwin's "Rhapsody in Blue." More annoyingly, middlebrow artworks swiped ideas and techniques from high art, then sanded off the spiky edges in order to attract an untrained audience. Dwight Macdonald invoked Thornton Wilder's *Our Town*, which employed Brechtian theatrical techniques to tell a jes' folks tale, and *The Old Man and the Sea*, a simplification of Hemingway's faux-naïf style ready-made for the Book of the Month Club. Mary McCarthy targeted Wilder's *Skin of Our Teeth* for installing "an elaborate system of mystification" that sought to "persuade the audience that it is witnessing a complex and difficult play, while what is really being shown on the stage is of a childish and almost painful naiveté."

True, the new media had disseminated the great achievements of the past more widely than ever before. Recordings and broadcasts of classical music, films about painting and theater, radio and magazine discussions of art and literature were now part of everyday life in America. Faulkner and Joyce were available in cheap editions. But this greater accessibility didn't guarantee understanding. According to legend, after finishing *Fantasia* Disney exclaimed, "Gee, this'll *make* Beethoven!" The same film turned Stravinsky's ritual of virgin sacrifice into a battle of dinosaurs. Middlebrow taste made crude art smooth, hard art easy.

Nervous about falling out of style, the middlebrow mind tried to keep up with the contemporary avant-garde. A lowbrow magazine would simply ignore Jackson Pollock's drip paintings or (if it was *Mad*) satirize them. By contrast, *Life*'s famous 1949 profile of the artist anxiously responds to the challenge of highbrow taste. Pollock is "a shining new phenomenon of American art" and may become "the greatest American painter of the century." Yet there's no attempt to explain why his work is significant. The work's value is appraised in cash terms (one painting is worth one hundred dollars a foot), and the results are mocked, timidly. Against the critics' praise is set the verdict of the common man. "He has also won a following among his own neighbors in the village of Springs, N.Y., who amuse themselves by trying to decide what his paintings are about. His grocer bought one which he identifies for bewildered visiting salesmen as an aerial view of Siberia." *Life* has hedged its bets (he *might* be great) while allowing a reader to say, "Aw, hell, my kid could paint that."

For such reasons, many intellectuals decided that while lowbrow culture was a danger, the real foe was middlebrow. The 1952 *Partisan Review* symposium identified the threat: "Do you think that American middlebrow culture has grown more powerful in this decade? In what relation does this middlebrow tendency stand to serious writing—does it threaten it or bolster it?" If lowbrow culture ignores high art, middlebrow betrays it.

There were obvious problems with conceiving mass culture as a united front of lowbrow and middlebrow. What about the great popular arts of earlier eras? Dickens, Poe, Tolstoy, Twain, and many others taken as high artists today wrote for popular audiences. What in our age prevented a widely beloved play or painting or novel from being good, even great? Then there was the issue of bad faith, as Auden noted: "Whenever the word Masses is used, we must read the words 'myself in weaker moments.'"

Hollywood, the Worst of Low and Middle

At the core of mass culture lay Hollywood movies. T. S. Eliot had already denounced "the encroachment of the cheap and rapid-breeding cinema," and by the 1940s no American could ignore films.

They were everywhere. Although Hollywood cut back production somewhat during the war years, many theaters ran double features, and most changed their bills two or three times a week. Hits were revived and recirculated. In cities energized by war work, some theaters were open twenty-four hours a day. Now that people had more money to spend, attendance surged. In this age before television, eighty-five to ninety million Americans, about 60 percent of the population, went to the movies each week. Today it's about twenty-five million a week, within a much larger population.

The mass media carried synergy and recycling to a new level. A novel (published in hardback, reprinted in paperback) could become a movie (promoted in magazines, with product tie-ins), then a radio show. The cult of stars grew, with popular actors constantly visible on billboards and in magazine ads. After *Gone with the Wind*, a best seller like *The Robe* or *Forever Amber* stirred frantic anticipation of the movie to come. Producers bought rights to books before publication, and studios commissioned books and plays so they could be turned into movies.

What was a poor intellectual to do? Back in the 1920s the critic Gilbert Seldes had championed slapstick comedy as a mixture of folk art and quasi-avant-garde challenges to genteel taste. But that was before Hollywood had turned filmmaking into a factory driven by finance capital and pumping out formulaic stories. After D. W. Griffith, Charles Chaplin, and Erich von Stroheim—the touchstones for all intellectuals interested in film—there was little to like in the studio product. Foreign lands had provided fine German films, notably *The Cabinet of Dr. Caligari*, and Soviet masterworks, above all *Potemkin*; but Nazism and Stalinism had stamped out those creative impulses. Dwight Macdonald denounced Soviet sound cinema as a form of kitsch at least as sinister as Hollywood's.

American intellectuals were hard-pressed to find much to admire in current cinema. Some tried to study the Hollywood film as a reflection of the American character or persistent myths of romance and getting rich. Alternatively, the films could mirror social anxieties. One eager critic writing for the *New Masses* found *The Cat People* (1942) deeply symbolic: "Its dark monster personifies the lurking terrors of a world crisis not understood." With few exceptions, however, the product of the studios was unrewarding as art. What wasn't lowbrow belonged firmly to the middle (*Wilson, The White Cliffs of Dover, Mrs. Miniver, The Best Years of Our Lives*).

After the war, André Bazin and other French critics would start to forge an aesthetic of the Hollywood sound cinema, but American writers did not think so abstractly. Ferguson, Agee, Farber, and Tyler worked more pragmatically to search out creativity in their time. All shared a trust in the standard story of the evolution of film art, from Griffith through the silent masters to René Clair in the early sound era. Yet they weren't hobbled by nostalgia; they reacted with immediacy to the cinema of their moment.

They set themselves apart from the larger debates of their age through shrewd flanking strategies. They largely avoided declaring political allegiance. Ferguson, recalled Alfred Kazin, "laughed at all revolutionary intellectuals as impossible utopians and fantasists." Agee once declared himself a Communist "by sympathy and conviction" but in the next breath attacked the worker idolatry of Soviet propaganda. Farber had, according to reports, tried to sign up with the Communist Party in the 1930s, but he didn't join the print polemics except to note as often as possible the plight of African American citizens. Tyler seems to have been nonaligned as well, although he indulged in occasional caustic asides about Hollywood's social commitment. He noted of *Meet John Doe*, "At this point in planetary affairs, American democracy becomes the theoretical right to hold a job and vote every four years for a new president."

Although Ferguson, Agee, and Farber wrote for left-liberal publications, they often went out of their way to support films that would be considered retrograde. Ferguson noted that a piece of hokum could be "very true in parts," while "the Great Social Document of the age" may "never stick for a minute." In a famous review, at the height of American solidarity with the Soviet defense of the homeland, Farber charged the Russian war film *The Rainbow* (1944) with naked cruelty. He also declared *The Birth of a Nation*, despite its outrageous bigotry, the greatest film yet made.

Likewise, all four critics finessed the mass culture controversy. You can find some snobbish asides about middlebrow culture here and there (Farber later charged that Agee was a middlebrow critic), and Agee and Tyler did flirt with calling some Hollywood films folk art. Basically, though, they didn't fight on that terrain. Agee spoke out against the "priggishness" of social scientists' critiques of thrillers like *The Big Sleep*. Perhaps these movies did "mirror" society, he admitted, but denunciation of American cinema productions as social symptoms missed the fact that such films were "relatively intelligent, accurate at least to something in the world, and entertaining."

> I realize also that on its most careful level, as practiced by Dr. Siegfried Kracauer or Barbara Deming, this sort of analysis is of interest

and value, dubious as I am about a good deal of it. But to me the most sinister thing that happened during the movie year [1947] was just this kind of analysis.

He was worried that these bleak cultural diagnoses were being seized on by "club women and the nastier kinds of church pressure groups." Ferguson, Farber, and Tyler would have agreed.

Culture in the Totally Administered Society

If under present conditions we cannot stop the ruthless expansion of mass-culture, the least we can do is keep apart and refuse its favors.

PHILIP RAHV, 1952

More generally, all four critics seemed to understand that the best way to show that American cinema had artistic dimensions was to present their case in precise, urgent, sometimes giddy prose. They were connoisseurs, making distinctions and discriminations of fine degree. And they found God, or the devil, in the details. In mounting those lines of defense, they risked condemnation by the most intellectually intimidating critic of the culture industry, the German émigré Theodor W. Adorno.

Adorno believed that in modern times, true art could only present itself as opposed to easy reception. Traditionally, an artwork aimed for totality, but the triumph of capitalism had made the harmony sought by classic art impossible. Even the very greatest achievements would reveal traces of contesting social forces. (One Adorno article on Beethoven is titled "Alienated Masterpiece: The *Missa Solemnis*.") By the twentieth century, the true artist could express only the *inability* to achieve harmony. Art's value lies "in those traits in which the discrepancy emerges, in the necessary failure of the passionate striving for identity." A formal dissonance in the artwork reveals its refusal to reconcile itself to capitalist demands. Some modernist art, such as Schoenberg's atonal pieces and Kafka's novels, achieved this refusal, but even much avant-garde music, painting, and literature fell short of bearing witness, in its very form and texture, to the crisis of life under high capitalism.

The Culture Industry, as characterized in Adorno and Max Hork-heimer's *Dialectic of Enlightenment*, becomes the ultimate expression of authoritarian rationality. As companies crank out commodities, so do Hollywood, Broadway, and Tin Pan Alley pump out synthetic artworks. Mass art's smooth surfaces are a grotesque parody of the unity struggled for by the great artists of the past. Form and content are harmonized in an ersatz, conformist way, and everything is tailored to easy pickup. The music "does the listening for the listener." Virtually by definition, the entertainment industry couldn't create art of value.

This is too brief an account of the Culture Industry thesis, but two points are especially relevant to our film critics. Adorno argues that the popular artwork concentrates not on the whole but on the part. Classic artists struggled to find a unity specific to each piece, but mass culture has made overall formats—the three-act play, the formulaic movie plot, the pop song—so generic that the only strong effects arise from isolated moments. An arresting plot twist or a sudden chord change has a brief impact. But by slotting itself into the set pattern, the little jolt simply confirms the validity of the prefabricated format.

Surely, though, there are major differences among these products? No two pop songs or movie melodramas are identical, and new styles emerge from time to time. Here comes the second point. Adorno claims that the differences we detect are fake. Each product of mass culture is "pseudo-individualized."

For one thing, the innovations are still very limited; jazz, Adorno wrote, is confined by its harmonic and metric schemes. Moreover, even innovation tends to confirm the standardized format. "The constant need to produce new effects (which must conform to the old pattern) serves merely as another rule to increase the power of the conventions." Adorno suggests that in jazz a "wrong" note is registered momentarily as a fresh detail, but the listener's ear immediately corrects it. As for film, "Orson Welles is forgiven all his offences against the usages of the craft because, as calculated rudeness, they confirm the validity of the system all the more zealously."

There's no escape. Just as one automobile or one breakfast cereal uses trivial differences to stand out from the competition, so too do songs and stories. Forms are formulas, novelties are minor and fleeting, and any deviations confirm the norm. Our four critics, by distinguishing subtly between this film and that, by focusing on scenes or details, have fallen into the mass culture trap.

Today it's easy to call this position humorless (no gags in genuine art) and elitist (everyone's a sucker but me) and to insist that those who write favorably about mass culture are on the side of right: the People. But this is just labeling. What if Adorno and Horkheimer's diagnosis is correct?

Perhaps there's no arguing with Culture Industry accounts like this on their own terms. They open too many escape hatches. Point to a film that exhibits what you take to be rich form, and the skeptic will say, "Call that complex? It's just a variant on the same old thing." Point to a ripe detail in a scene, and you'll be told it's just pseudodifferentiation. If *Ulysses* and Schoenberg's *Erwartung* are your prime examples of valid art, *His Girl Friday* isn't going to measure up, let alone *Rhapsody Rabbit*.

It's more productive, I think, to point out some historical and conceptual difficulties. For example, Adorno and Horkheimer generalize too fast from the model of heavy industry and mass production. It's true that the culture "industry" utilizes division of labor and hierarchies of control. But this isn't specific to modern capitalism, as we know from artists' ateliers in earlier times. Titian, Brueghel the Younger, Rembrandt, and other painters supervised employees who specialized in rendering certain patches of a canvas. Those workshops, in a prefiguration of movie facilities, were called studios.

Going further, film production can't be standardized to the degree that high-output manufacture is. It's an error to consider Hollywood an "assembly line" system. No two movies are as much alike as two Fords rolling off the line at River Rouge. Hollywood employs an *artisanal* mode of production, in which each worker adds something distinctive to the result, and the "product" is a complex blend of overlapping and crisscrossing contributions. Marx called this mode of production "serial manufacture." Instead of rigid standardization, differentiation is built into the system, and the differences aren't all blueprinted via central command.

Another difficulty comes, I think, when we recognize just how stringent are Adorno's and Horkheimer's standards for valuable art. The bar is set excruciatingly high. "Telling a story," Adorno noted in 1954, "means having something *special* to say, and that is precisely what is prevented by the administered world, by standardization and eternal sameness." So fresh and authentic stories are impossible? Most of us aren't prepared to narrow our experience so drastically.

More theoretically, Adorno's insistence that the true modern artwork must be sui generis, related to tradition only in labyrinthine dialectical ways, seems to me implausible. It puts him close to Benedetto Croce's view that each artwork is irreducibly unique. By contrast, I'd argue that artworks good or bad, classic or avant-garde, owe a great deal, and quite openly, to norms, styles, genres, and other traditions. It doesn't take anything away from modernism's innovations to recognize that artists like Joyce, Picasso, Woolf, Conrad, Stravinsky, and Schoenberg "took the next step" beyond the state of play at the time. Where does radical change shade off into pseudodifferentiation?

And it would have come as news to Orson Welles to learn from Adorno that Hollywood had "forgiven all his offences."

Toward a Criticism of Popular Art

If you like to keep warm in your neighborhood theatre these days or have to review movies for a living, you can find something good in any film.

MANNY FARBER, 1946

Did my Rhapsodes read Adorno or Horkheimer? *Dialectic of Enlightenment* wasn't translated into English until 1972, but the Frankfurt School's ideas were circulating in their milieu. (A 1941 Adorno essay on popular music influenced Macdonald's "Theory of 'Popular Culture'" essay.) In any case, my critics outflanked the mass culture debates by simply diving, quite self-consciously, into popular material—something very few intellectuals were willing to do. The result is a sensitivity to nuances within popular art that we seldom find in the Frankfurt School writers.

Plunging into the material had a particular importance at this moment. During the 1940s, criticism became technical to a degree never seen before. I haven't found any piece by Adorno or Horkheimer that troubles to analyze closely any product of the Culture Industry. Writing on Mahler or Berg, Adorno gets somewhat concrete, but he never dismantles a simple jitterbug tune. As a "social philosopher" rather than a critic, he produces a general denunciation that exempts him from looking closely. One has only to compare Adorno's vague philippics about jazz with Ferguson's 1930s pieces. The latter's famous appreciation of Bix Beiderbecke shows his technical knowledge without showing it off, draws pointed comparisons with other musicians, and captures what is both traditional and new about jazz.

He played a full easy tone, no forcing, faking, or mute tricks, no glissando to cover unsure attack or vibrato to fuzz over imprecisions of pitch—it all had to be in the music. And the clear line of that music is something to wonder at. You see, this is the sort of thing that is almost wholly improvised, starting from a simple theme and taking off from that into a different and unpredictable melodic line, spontaneous, personal—almost a new tune but still shadowing the old one, anchored in its chord sequence. Obviously, without lyric invention and a perfect instinct for harmony, this is no go for a minute, let alone chorus after chorus, night after night.

Adorno's refusal to ground his critique in close analysis stands out in contrast to what was happening in the American art world of the time. Most apparent was the flourishing of the New Criticism in literary studies. During the 1930s Cleanth Brooks, Robert Penn Warren, and others in America had picked up ideas of "close reading" from I. A. Richards and William Empson in England. Those ideas were disseminated to universities across America in Brooks and Warren's 1938 textbook *Understanding Poetry* and its successor *Understanding Fiction* (1943). Literary history, the survey of authors and their times, was being displaced by the scrutiny of a single poem or story as an isolated work. In calling his time "an age of criticism," Randall Jarrell complained that this urge for technical analysis was sapping the energies of both poets and critics, but it has become a central way of understanding literature.

Critics of the visual arts were developing vivacious analyses of painters' strategies. Erle Loran's *Cezanne's Composition* (1943), for example, revealed large-scale principles of design underlying paintings that may have seemed a jumble of colors and planes. In the context of weekly reviewing, Clement Greenberg, Harold Rosenberg, Meyer Schapiro, and others probed details of color and paint handling. Farber, in his guise as art critic, was positively fussy in anatomizing the layout of a Léger and the candy-box palette of a Chagall.

Musicology, long geared to rigorous analysis, was finding new layers of patterning in both classic and modern works. Heinrich Schenker's formalism of earlier decades provided a basis for this inquiry. The rise of various musical avant-gardes employing complex compositional procedures, as in serialism, demanded ever more sharply focused studies of form. While Adorno and Hanns Eisler were denouncing kitsch music in film soundtracks, musicologists were dissecting *Objective Burma!*, *The Strange Love of Martha Ivers*, *The Best Years of Our Lives*, and other scores.

Our four critics didn't, indeed couldn't, conduct such microscopic analysis of movies. But they did burrow into the fine grain of American films to an unprecedented degree. For example, Agee, when he started writing his *Nation* column in 1942, declared that he would "feel no apology for whatever my eyes tell me." Here he is praising Huston for a moment in *The Treasure of the Sierra Madre* (1948).

> *Treasure's* intruder is killed by bandits; the three prospectors come to identify the man they themselves were on the verge of shooting. Bogart, the would-be tough guy, cocks one foot up on a rock and tries to look at the corpse as casually as if it were fresh-killed game.

2.1 *The Treasure of the Sierra Madre* (1948).

Tim Holt, the essentially decent young man, comes past behind him and, innocent and unaware of it, clasps his hands as he looks down, in the respectful manner of a boy who used to go to church. Walter Huston, the experienced old man, steps quietly behind both, leans to the dead man as professionally as a doctor to a patient and gently rifles him for papers.

Thanks to steady looking, Agee can argue that the film has a novelistic power to delineate character, but without words, just through framing and physical action—in other words, through the "clean, direct" expression that Ferguson found in American studio cinema. That terseness finds its echo in Agee's style, which packs characterizing details into adjectives and homely metaphors; one phrase, "a boy who used to go to church," sketches a man's life history.

Just as the New Critics punctured generalizations about poetry by exposing the nuances of syntax and metaphor, Ferguson, Agee, Farber, and Tyler provide, in a roundabout way, an answer to the critics of mass culture. Through their precision of observation and the contagious enthusiasm of their rhetoric, they showed that blanket denunciations of popular entertainment missed areas of vitality and creativity, tendencies toward expressive form and emotional force. Sometimes those accomplishments fit the canons of high art, sometimes not. And at moments these critics traced the general outlines of an aesthetic specific to the Hollywood sound cinema.

Not all intellectuals condemned the culture industry utterly. The art historian Erwin Panofsky claimed that films were a true instance of folk art. From the University of Chicago, Mortimer Adler produced an Aristotelian account of the motion picture "as a work of fine art" and argued in nearly seven hundred pages that "the technique of the motion picture is vastly superior to the critical acumen of its commentators."

Within the social sciences David Riesman proposed that modern mass culture housed a great many levels, each with its own criteria and artistic ambitions. He dared to claim that there could be good art at every level. Moreover, the audience was often more aware of the qualities on display than the critics were. In a gesture that anticipates today's academic study of fandom and taste communities, Riesman proposed this:

> The various mass audiences are not so manipulated as often supposed: they fight back, by refusing to "understand," by selective interpretation, by apathy. Conformity there surely is, but we cannot assume its existence from the standardization of the commodities themselves (in many instances a steadily diminishing standardization) without knowledge of how individuals and groups interpret the commodities and endow them with meanings.

Individuals and groups used media products in a variety of ways, Riesman claimed. The individual's peer groups might even set up taste structures that could run against the ones offered by media industries. Jazz aficionados, both amateurs and critics, discerned styles and genres not acknowledged by the record companies. In a quiet knock on the high-art standards of literary academics, he suggests that "taste exchange" among fans and critics constitutes "the Newer Criticism." He might almost have been talking about the Internet.

Or about my four writers. If we think of Ferguson, Agee, Farber, and Tyler scooping out of mass art something they could defend, we might consider each a peer group of one. They undertook to test their personal histories and "taste structures" against the churn of commercial cinema. What they devised, suitably sharpened by the pressure of their writing styles, were personalized, powerful versions of a Newer Criticism.

3 *Otis Ferguson*
THE WAY OF THE CAMERA

Of my four critics, Ferguson remains the least known today. That's a pity, because he was an exceptional writer. He had some of the pungency of H. L. Mencken, but he didn't indulge in the Sage of Baltimore's exhausting rhetorical barrages. Ferguson wrote in the laconic, wiseacre idiom of the generation who faced the turmoil of the 1930s and who knew the lessons of Ring Lardner, Ernest Hemingway, and Gertrude Stein. Jazz inflected his prose, as did the pulse of the movies, which by the time he started reviewing had finally learned to talk properly.

The result was wondrous. His style ranged from roughneck slang to tender lyricism, anticipating Farber in the one and Agee in the other. But he blended them and could turn on a dime.

> [The producers of the Russian film *Broken Shoes*] fail to see that truth is not a formulaic concoction, to be thinly coated with something glucose and fired into the market like buckshot; but rather a quality of light, effective only when inherent in the material and allowed to play naturally through it.

With a single phrase (*fired into the market like buckshot*) the passage swerves away from mawkishness, giving sincerity to the final uplift. Just as everyday conversations hop from high metaphor to curse words, Ferguson could jump registers.

> Harry Carey is as wonderful and right as ever—he is cast as the country doctor and damned if I wouldn't let him operate right now, though as he says, "Lady, the things I don't know you could herd like cows."

He could draw things out fine with absurdly consistent parallel clauses:

> [*Riptide* is] the story of a lord who married a lady thinking her true, but later thinking her false (though true she still was), and then

thinking her true again (she having by this time and out of boredom become mildly false) and then finding her false (though to be
sure she couldn't keep it up and was by this time true again) and
finally discovering that she was his wife after all (which everybody
had known all along). In the face of which Herbert Marshall and
Norma Shearer are powerless.

He could pull off an epigram too, as when he talks of Tallulah Bankhead
in a stage production of *The Little Foxes*.

> Even in a part which allows her to dominate a play, she should not try
> to be Maurice Evans, and neither, I suppose, should Maurice Evans.

He can be as familiar with you as he likes. On *Yellow Jack*:

> [Robert Montgomery] has a chance to swagger and get a bit tough
> and there are fine scenes horsing around with the men—I knew a
> sergeant of Marines like that once, damn him.

> I know you can get more fact and less fancy out of the same two
> hours in a library, if you know where to look. And now all of those
> who have spent two hours in a library digging up the record of Dr.
> Reed will please lift up the right hand. You see.

The grammar is usually correct, but sometimes you can't be sure.

> [*Espionage Agent*] has to take a stand too, and so its throat is full
> of the demand that Congress do something about something. I'm
> afraid it won't do and I'm afraid we are in for a lot more of and
> worse than the same.

His *ands*, you see, are booby traps. They'll be leading you along in nice
parade formation, and then you strike a trip wire.

> From being allowed only sulks or smiles (and the director took his
> pick), she has got herself a whole style of giving out, as in radia-
> tion, ranges of feeling and being she never had to learn because
> they can't be learned but just have to be there, like elements, and
> presently I feel I am going to get quite silly about Ginger Rogers.

Sometimes just a comma does the job.

> Jack Teagarden (otherwise Jackson, Mister Jack, Mister T. Bill Gate, etc.) is one of the really high men in the jazz collection, I'll tell you more about it.

And he can mount a fine barbed insult.

> The more specious [*Holiday*] appeared, the more I noticed and resented Katharine being Hepburn till it hurt, and the Stewart-Buchman writing job that encouraged her in this to points where that flat metallic voice is driven into your head like needles.

As the first long-running film critic in a national intellectual weekly, Ferguson enjoyed more space for his provocations than did his rivals, those sad short-termers and half-hearted reporters working elsewhere. For them he had undisguised disdain; he knew he was the best. Throughout he maintained an element of boyish bravado. He praised movies showing men at work, and he seemed determined to write as a tough (but tender) guy should. ("Virility" would become a term of high praise for Agee and Farber.) It was as if Ferguson set out to disprove *New Yorker* editor Harold Ross's claim that movie reviewing was for "women and fairies."

Ferguson showed, week after week, how to talk about popular art with sincerity, enthusiasm, precision, and a sardonic humor that owed nothing to the brittle epigrams of the Algonquin Round Table. In just a few years, he changed American film criticism. His legacy has a linear simplicity. Without Ferguson, probably no Agee and surely no Farber. Without Agee and Farber, no Pauline Kael and Andrew Sarris. Without Kael and Sarris, no modern film criticism. Perhaps worst of all, without Ferguson, no Ferguson.

Swing Time

He was born in 1907 and grew up on a Massachusetts farm. He left high school to join the navy, came home, and finished high school. At Clark University he won a student writing award sponsored by the *New Republic*. After graduation in 1933 the magazine hired him as what he called a utility player; he reviewed books, theater, and movies, with occasional essays on jazz performers. His first film review appeared in 1934. He served as well as assistant editor to Malcolm Cowley, the urbane ruler of the arts section.

Ferguson continued with the magazine until early 1942, when he enlisted in the Merchant Marine. He was killed in the Mediterranean in 1943. A radio-guided bomb struck his ship when he was alone in the ship's mess, drinking coffee. By the time of his death Manny Farber had replaced him as film reviewer for the *New Republic*, and James Agee had started writing movie pieces for the *Nation* and *Time*.

The *New Republic*, founded as a progressive magazine in 1916, housed some writers on the far left, including Stalinist sympathizers and fellow travelers like Cowley, but there were moderates and Roosevelt Democrats in the house as well. Ferguson added a combustible element to the political debates: his personality.

Talking out of the side of his mouth, he seemed to have a perpetual chip on his shoulder. He presented himself as the tough guy who came up the hard way, who spent four years at sea and worked his way through college. Had the *New Republic* not picked up a (rather bad) piece of dialect reportage in his junior year at Clark, he might have wound up, in those Depression years, staying on as a pinboy in a bowling alley.

An anti-intellectual intellectual, he boiled with resentment at the Fitzgeralds and Edmund Wilsons who had passed easily from prep school to the Ivy League and then to secure berths in Manhattan publishing. So he disrupted office life with pranks and obscene puns. He wrote with a bottle of whiskey at his elbow. He dressed in defiance of taste; Kazin recalls him striding through Union Square in a black shirt, yellow tie, and bright green sport jacket. Kazin, a friend but no admirer, suspected that Ferguson infiltrated bohemia "out of curiosity and mockery, almost as a joke."

He could unleash indignation at will. Leaving his post for war duty, he looked back in anger, bemoaning the absence of serious film criticism by casually insulting other critics by name. He castigated songwriters and band arrangers who after Pearl Harbor dusted off sugary war tunes for the new times. "A man has to make a living. But this boozy and whipped-up patriotism is what I would call making a living the dirty way." As for the need to keep up morale, as he looked back at the Great War, he saw only "the morale of those who were having just the hell of a time hating the Hun from easy chairs and making more easy money than they'd ever seen in their lives." Ferguson may have spurned Marxist theory, but he had the primal resentment of a roofer watching the suburbanites keep bankers' hours.

It wasn't only the writing. In person he was truculent and sardonic. The critic whose god-word was "sweet" could be harsh and bullying. His paradigm of conversation seems to have been the quarrel. "If you said 'white' to him," Cowley recalled, "Otis said 'black.' If you made the mistake of saying 'genius,' quick as a flash he answered 'phony.'" For a man who hated war, he seems to have been awfully bellicose. Any casual disagreement could escalate into a shouting match. A secretary at the magazine recalled him wielding "really wounding insults, the veins standing out on his forehead."

Like many who vent their anger on their subordinates, he had unpredictable spurts of kindness. After his death, the magazine printed tributes from two young men—one a writer, the other a jazz novice—who had been encouraged by Ferguson. Even the secretary he berated found him at her sickbed, making drinks and "waiting on you hand and foot, tender as a mother." She added, "You'd realize you were fonder of him than anyone else in the world."

Perhaps his *New Republic* staffmates forgave him because he galvanized the place. Kazin again:

> He jumped and twitched with the restlessness of a jazz man, and from the moment he came up to you in the corridor, you felt yourself shaking with him, knees, hands and arms jangling in rhythm to some private tune; his mind seemed to be constantly dancing and darting, moving and shaking.

Kazin was not alone in attributing Ferguson's nervous physicality to jazz. This music gave his spirit a lift (another god-word) and exemplified how beauty could be born of barely controlled bursts of energy. Jess Stacy, pianist for Benny Goodman's band, remembered him as a drinking buddy but also an obsessive. "Otis realized the importance of the piano in a big band, and when he came to hear us he'd sit practically under the piano on the bandstand, which annoyed the hell out of Benny, which pleased us."

Ferguson's music criticism centered on swing. Radio and records made big band jazz the dominant form of pop music, as central to the lives of millions as movies were. Ferguson believed the new bands developed the "easy-ride quality" that had been in the background of Dixieland and the blues, then pulled it through a richer harmonic structure. The danceable rhythms and clear-cut formal framework of swing still permitted soloists to soar, as Ferguson's favorites Beiderbecke and Teagarden could.

Ferguson barhopped with players and went on the road with Goodman's band. He visited clubs and tried in his prose to capture how the music seized its listeners.

> When Teddy Hill's men begin swinging the last choruses of the specialty number "Christopher Columbus," with those driving brass figures and the reed section going down to give it body the dancers forget dancing and flock around the stand ten deep, to register the time merely with their bones and muscles, standing there in one place with their heads back and letting it flow over them like water—invitation (and the waltz be damned) to blow the man down. The floor shakes and the place is a dynamo room, with the smoky air pushing up in steady waves, and swing it, men, get off, beat it out, and in a word play that thing. It's a music deaf men could hear.

Ferguson wrote mostly about white bands and musicians, but that wasn't due to prejudice. Ferguson admired Louis Armstrong, Duke Ellington, and Fletcher Henderson, and one of his best essays reports on an all-night stay in a Harlem club. But because of segregation and the decline of black clubs during the Depression, he had less chance to hear black music live. During his last year on the *New Republic*, he published a beginner's guide to collecting jazz records. He suggested starting with Bing Crosby and Benny Goodman and Red Norvo before moving to "the raw stuff as it came up the Mississippi from New Orleans." That list was dominated by Armstrong: "You could cover a warehouse floor with his records, and most of them would make good listening." But his recommendations still reflect his preference for "the full-band idiom," music built around a team of extraordinary players who take turns as soloists.

Ferguson worked on two books on jazz, but neither was finished. He planned a collection of his jazz essays, but he fell out with the publisher and didn't bother to find another. There's an intriguing congruence between Ferguson's writing habits and the protean, spur-of-the-moment quality of jazz performance. Like Agee and Farber, he needed deadlines in order to finish pieces. After writing all night, he would rush to the office and make final changes at the typesetter's side. Perhaps this was Ferguson's form of improvisation: a piece was never complete, was always open to a new twist or grace note.

In Defense of Soothing Imbecility

We expect liveliness, however forced or strained, in our movie criticism. A review may begin with the critic remembering something from child-hood, or a first visit to a movie like the new release or, if the writer sits high enough on the food chain, a first meeting with a revered director. Even when things aren't so autobiographical, we expect our critics to be chatty, quick, and "passionate" in a distinctive way. And the review must include the first-person pronoun, abundantly.

When Ferguson came on the scene, New York arts journalism wasn't so conversational. The high-level reviewer of art, literature, and drama was an urbane cosmopolitan with a dry wit who expressed himself (almost always a himself) in the most measured terms. Even if something was exciting, the reviewer kept his poise. Blame and praise were distributed judiciously. Polite distance ruled. You might throw in an occasional *I*, but *we* and *us* and *our*, conveniently vague, settled reader and writer into adjacent easy chairs at the club.

For example, the Arts section of the *New Republic* sheltered Stark Young. For decades he was one of New York's most respected drama crit-ics. Today it is hard to see why. The chatty platitudes that fill his pages are set forth in prose as beige and lumpy as oatmeal.

> The whole procedure of Mr. Marc Blitzstein's opera, "The Cradle Will Rock," comes freshly across the footlights, and dull would he be of soul—antiquated red poetic rag as that may be to the Newist bull—who could pass by the living theatre here presented. It makes one proud, makes one swell, believing in the reality of talent and impetuosity, chances taken, and the assertion of vividness. The composer plays the piano . . . , the opera goes on scene by scene, the vignette events and graphic dramatics are clearly revealed. Great talent goes into this piece; you never nod, never try to send your thoughts elsewhere, never mistrust.

If you are still awake, I think you'll agree that this is resolutely unexcit-ing. With upper-tier reviewing dominated by this sort of drowsy murmur, it's not surprising that readers were drawn to a different kind of voice. On the same day that Young reviewed Blitzstein, Ferguson wrote this:

> One record-breaker predictable for 1938 is the fact that Warner Brothers has made a good musical: "Hollywood Hotel." You can

believe it or not, but the picture has Louella Parsons and Dick Powell; and the story is that familiar turkey about a young singer who makes good in Hollywood. Yet it's fresh and at times irresistible—it is even a musical comedy with comedy.

There are times when the referee counted up to at least seven on it.

In print, Ferguson made friendly references to Young, but those don't hide the strange incompatibilities. When Ferguson started at the *New Republic*, he was twenty-six and Young was fifty-two. Young was prominent in the Agrarian circle, a conservative group of southern intellectuals who tried to counter criticisms of sharecropping and lynchings with reminders of the radiant aristocracy that once graced the Old South. Ferguson cast his lot with Mencken, a demonic figure to the Agrarians.

These differences of age and pedigree matter, but I think the Young/Ferguson faceoff is settled by style. Imagine you are eager to learn arts journalism. You run your eye over a lead from Professor Young:

> With no touch of irony I must confess I feel a certain touch of shyness in writing of "Time and the Conways," for I do not know where I am with it.

One *touch* is enough, but two make us worry how "certain" the second is. By contrast, a Ferguson lead pitches across the plate, though with a screwball twist.

> David O. Selznick's colored-candy version of *The Adventures of Tom Sawyer* should make Mark Twain circulate in his grave like a trout in a creel—sentimentalist though the old boy was, partial though he was to the black-and-white, the character bromide.

Whose desk would you hang around?

Before Ferguson arrived, Young had reviewed some films, all of which he declared worthless as art. He had never seen one in which serious issues were treated with human significance. Still, Young admitted enjoying *Tarzan of the Apes* because "I like to relapse into something like a soothing imbecility."

Dilettantes from the theater world like Young were embarrassing enough, but even purported film specialists offered little promise. Ferguson's 1942 parting shot, "The Case of the Critics," complained that movie journalism had made almost no progress since he had started. In a burst of bad temper, he caricatured his colleagues as snobs and amateurs.

Clearly he went too far. One target, Richard Watts Jr., was a competent daily reviewer. As for the *Nation*'s William Troy, it's not hard to see why Ferguson jeered at him. Raised in Oak Park, Illinois, trained at Yale and Columbia, employed as a star professor at top colleges: Troy represented everything Ferguson resented. Yet Troy's academic turn of mind led him to appreciate the tragic overtones of *M* and the originality of "narratage" in *The Power and the Glory*. Troy didn't despise Hollywood, and within the few column inches he was allotted he could dash off illuminating points. He was no Ferguson, but he was no fool either.

Ferguson's jeremiad, broadly unfair as it was, made three valid complaints. First, all these writers and platforms deployed Standard Critic English—not as stupefying as Young's prose, but still flat and "obediently dull and uninformative." Ferguson, over eight years, had tried to shake things up through the power of his language.

Second, the critics didn't have personal conceptions of cinema. A good critic traffics in ideas and information as well as opinion. Through thinking about cinema's strongest achievements, a critic might arrive at some general and original notions about the art of the sound movie. Such notions Ferguson had in abundance.

Third, just before writing his "Case of the Critics," Ferguson had been to Hollywood. I think that seeing teamwork on a film set, no less neat and precise than that in a swing band, brought home to him how craft practices created expressive effects. His 1942 diatribe suggested that critics who had no interest in the nuts and bolts of their art form weren't worthy of it. "If [a movie critic] has the slightest conception of how movies are made and why, he will probably be given a job doing something else."

This Motion and This Air of Life

Writing for the *New Republic* didn't bias Ferguson toward films of leftish social commitment. He did cover a few Soviet paeans to the proletariat, but probably that was out of convenience: he lived in an apartment over a theater specializing in Russian imports. Above all, though, he demanded that a movie be engaging entertainment.

"I can see at the start that this film, *Lives of a Bengal Lancer*, is going to cause me a lot of grief, first because from a social point of view it is execrable, second, because it is a dashing sweat-and-leather sort of thing and I like it." Why like it? It is less about British colonialism and more about showing how men pull together, portraying "the rough satisfaction of combining finely with all the others to make the thing work, to go off smoothly." A few years later he found the film "just as politically incorrect and marvelous as ever." He asked that leftists "stop demanding a ten-reel feature on the Rise of Western Imperialism and look around to see what *can* be done with pictures."

Actually, what could be done with pictures *had* been done. Working in a popular art form, talented artisans had created a narrative cinema answering to a unique discipline. The best Hollywood films had shown that cinema was a storytelling medium committed to lowercase naturalism and crisp, efficient technique.

Ferguson started reviewing a little too late to cover *Footlight Parade* (1933), which is a pity: it perfectly instantiates the new talkie style he came to admire. Today we tend to remember the film for its concluding musical numbers, realized with Busby Berkeley's typical flamboyance. "Honeymoon Hotel," "By a Waterfall," and "Shanghai Lil" are practically minimovies, each flagrantly disregarding the space of the stage they're supposedly confined to. Yet they are actually three fat cherries on a delectable sundae.

What comes before the showstoppers is a feverish plot packed with reversals and double-crosses. In the film's first three minutes protagonist Chester Kent loses his job as a producer of stage musicals. Sixty seconds after that, his wife leaves him for Reno. A minute after that, a visit to a drugstore inspires him to create a new business: short-form prologues accompanying talking pictures, with the casts shipped from theater to theater. Applying the chain-store model to entertainment is the answer to his predicament, so forty seconds after being bound for the breadline, Chester is running a vast ensemble of singers and dancers. Every day he strains to come up with a new idea while contending with crooked partners, an assistant who betrays him, a spy who's slipping Chester's ideas to his competitor, a dirty-minded censor, a dyspeptic theater mogul, a producer's wife babying a protégé, a secretary who wants to be a hoofer, a crooner who wants the secretary, a gold digger fended off by the female assistant who loves Chester, and a cigar-chewing dance director who wails that he can't work in such chaos.

After the lugubrious rhythm of early talkies, the unrelenting momentum of *Footlight Parade* must have seemed torrential. Though the tempo recalls silent-film comedy, in those days the visual gags would likely have flown by as part of a chase. Here the twists and complications spring up in offices and rehearsal halls, with slamming doors and barked orders and interrupted auditions creating a deadline-pressured crescendo recalling *The Front Page* and other newspaper sagas.

No wonder that by the mid-1930s sheer artiness on the European silent model came to seem hollow and heavy. Ferguson used his review of *Three Songs of Lenin* as an occasion to deplore "pure cinema." Instead of discussing Vertov's film, he fills his column with a hypothetical city symphony, telling of desolate streets waking up to a fusillade of rapid editing. "You cut in the big dynamo wheels, all the wheels, all the powerhouses, wheels and wheels. Rah, *montage.*" The "advanced" style of the silent era had become an anachronism, as stale as a gavotte. With films like *Footlight Parade* studio cinema had created a new aesthetic appropriate to talking pictures.

Three months after *Footlight Parade* was released, Ferguson started reviewing, and very soon he noted that something was up.

> If there is any one thing that the movie people seem to have learned in the last few years, it is the art of taking some material—any material, it may be sound, it may be junky—and working it up until the final result is smooth, fast-moving, effortless. . . . Whoever started the thing in the first place, Hollywood has it now, and Hollywood speaks a different language.

Thanks to the new dramaturgy of the talkies, any novel or play, he realized, could now be molded into a fresh, sprightly shape. But how could one understand this new language?

Of all his attempts, this one is handiest, but it needs glossing.

> The real art of movies concentrates on getting the right story and the right actors, the right kind of production and then smoothing everything out. And after that, in figuring how each idea can be made true, how each action can be made to happen, how you cut and reverse-camera and remake each minute of action, and run it into a line afterward, like the motion in the ocean.

Most generally, Ferguson is defending what Hollywood had long called continuity. From the late 1910s on, popular filmic storytelling bent its energies toward flow. A film script was called a continuity. The woman who tended to the details of shooting was the continuity girl. The need to make props and lighting and positions constant from shot to shot was called continuity. And continuity editing created smooth match-cuts and unnoticeable changes of angle. Studio storytelling was continuity through and through.

What is the "right story"? It's a coherent tale that maintains a clear "line" (one of his favorite words). That line should drive forward rapidly but without fuss or jitter. Continuity, he says, "signifies that cumulative power of a story, or a statement of conflict, when it progresses from its elected point to its stern, inevitable end." This overall momentum isn't easy to attain; in Ferguson's view even *Citizen Kane* and *How Green Was My Valley* were too episodic.

The new style is partly a matter of exuberant tempo, a refusal of longueurs. In *Footlight Parade*, some scenes—not shots, whole scenes—run less than thirty seconds.

But speed alone isn't enough. The principle of continuity demands both overarching coherence and an easy progression from scene to scene. So *Footlight Parade* sets up its crisis—the need to produce three big prologues from scratch in three days—from the very start. During the early dialogue scenes, we hear melodies rehearsed offscreen; they'll return, full blast, in the big numbers at the end. Moment by moment, the film runs its scenes together with fast wipes and pitilessly rapid cause and effect. Chester's wife divorces him, he needs an aspirin, he visits a drugstore that sells aspirin cheap, and bingo: chain-store stage shows are born.

Who are the "right actors"? For Ferguson, Hollywood's glide-path storytelling depends on a certain naturalism of behavior and appearance. This isn't the Naturalism of Zola and Frank Norris or that of the Neorealist cinema to come from Italy. For Ferguson, naturalism is a felt accord with social life outside the movie house. Hollywood cinema, in its plays and players, can bring us the behavior of typical, fully realized human beings in their interchanges with others.

Better than the novel, the film can summon up the world we know, thanks to filmmakers and performers who "still remembered something of life as it appears to those who merely live it." So Ferguson can praise *Tom, Dick, and Harry* (1941) for mimicking what its audience will do when the lights come up: a couple leave the movie house, stop at a soda fountain, then go to a clearing where other couples neck. Some stars retained ties to the workaday world. Errol Flynn might be "about as expressive as the leg of a chair," but men like Pat O'Brien and James Cagney "were in so many instances a part of common life just yesterday that they haven't had time to forget it, dress it up, and bury it."

Ferguson was aware that many aspects of naturalism were mere con-

ventions. "Our estimate of what is natural shifts with each new stylization of it." Still, he thinks there is a constant texture of living that is
instantly recognizable, and filmmakers can weave that into a dramatic
plot. A film by Lang or Ford or Milestone wraps an engrossing story
around work routines, character exchanges, and "life in action and at
mess and horsing around."

> When [the miners of *Black Fury*] were working, or chewing the fat,
> or drinking their pitiful nickels away in the bar they were no strang-
> ers to you. . . . [They were] so cleverly worked into a story-pattern
> of cause and result, environment and hopes, that they were neither
> symbols nor foreigners but people you knew and hoped the best
> of. You knew their work and their dinner table, their mean streets
> and threadbare pleasures; and everything about it was simple and
> just-so, through the medium of the most complex and expensive
> art on earth.

The word Ferguson finds for this quality: *honest.*

This is all a product of teamwork, and Ferguson knew very well that
the best things in a scene may come from anyone involved in the production. Still, as viewers we never really know whom to thank for what, so we
use the shorthand of attributing faults or beauties to the director. And
sometimes it's obvious. Thanks to John Ford, the sweating men on Dry
Tortuga in *The Prisoner of Shark Island* come to life through "a shrewd care
for the pitch and speed of every move, every detail." Capra and Hitchcock,
Wyler and Welles, Hawks and Lang: Ferguson saw that those directors
whom later generations would salute as old masters were steering the
sound cinema where it ought to go.

The smooth, naturalistic storytelling that Ferguson valued is incarnated in another quality, one as important for him as for the pioneering
tastemaker Gilbert Seldes. Movies should move. Static talking scenes
are of less value than drama translated into action. This doesn't mean
that every scene must be a fight or a chase, only that the scene should
project a flow of physical activity in which skillful performers realize
the story concretely. To go back to *Footlight Parade*, the spark is James
Cagney's performance as Chester Kent. Cagney drives the scenes forward
with pint-size roars, wrist-snapped commands, a hitched-up rump, and
heedlessly fast line readings. His conversations are physical confronta-
tions. He twists his crooked partners' lapels, hustles his backer into an

office, sweeps along platoons of chorus girls, shoves his dance director down on all fours to imitate a prowling cat. This feral pug was made for the new Hollywood.

Melodrama, musicals, gangster films, comedy light or slapstick—all find their ultimate expression in charged motion, big or small. For Ferguson the stateroom scene in *A Night at the Opera* sits at one extreme.

> Groucho has just squeezed into a third-class stateroom with a trunk big enough to hold two brothers and a tenor, who pop out of it as soon as the door is wedged shut, and then people begin to pile in— manicurists, cleaning maids, retired majors, stewards with trays, the engineer's assistant, the engineer looking for him. They begin to get about seven deep and the laws of physics are insulted right and left, Groucho still the host, sarcastic and regal with a cigar, the other two still swarming up the chambermaids, everything still piling up and bulging the walls until just the second when the rich matron, never so outraged but blackmailed into it, sweeps along to her assignation with Groucho and arrives square in front of the door, which breaks out like a shot and they all spill out clear across the ship, like a tubful of blueberries.

At the other extreme is a slight moment ("a minor thing, too") in *The Little Foxes*:

> Herbert Marshall has come out to lean his weak fury against the bannister. Bette Davis has come home from the battle-line, entering from the door across the space below, preoccupied and busy with gloves and stuff, to take five steps, six, seven (we know he is there, we are waiting) and another step and, *stop*. The dramatic part of the scene lifts up like a full chord in the orchestra, and we think, it is this woman who has looked up with her hard nervous eyes to find this object of hate.

In the final phase of production, Ferguson notes, the cutter "remakes" each bit of movement and runs it "into a clear line." Many in the 1930s clung to the idea of editing as the creative essence of cinema. Ferguson's notion of editing is in accord with Hollywood's practice. Editing doesn't create the action, but it gives it a graceful shape. Editing isn't world-conquering montage but a final tuning. Ferguson notes, for instance, that in a dialogue it's clumsy to simply cut from one speaker to another,

3.1 *The Little Foxes* (1941).

line by line (as is too often done today). "Being a director consists exactly in knowing how to break this up, to keep interest shifting to stress the reaction to a line more sharply than the face saying it. This is what gives a picture life."

All of these dynamic qualities, story and performance and pacing and editing, didn't appear on the scene immediately. Ferguson accepts that the first years of talkies had been a setback for artistic cinema, but once dialogue became integrated with images, and once filmmakers had figured out tempo and fitting details into the whole, big changes could happen.

André Bazin famously dated the crystallization of "classical" storytelling to 1939 with *Stagecoach*. Ferguson, with his love of vernacular comedy, set the turning point back in 1934, his first year on the job, with *Sing and Like It* and *The Thin Man* and *Twentieth Century* and *The Gay Divorcee* and above all *It Happened One Night*. At that point an elegant unity of story and style was achieved. "The movies had arrived at a new ease and maturity in form, a form that became most distinguishable in that it had tempered all effects from wipe-dissolves to Clark Gable into a steady line of clear motion."

By the mid-1930s, a unique method of audiovisual storytelling had been mastered by the classic studio cinema, and in a form that was correctly named: *moving* pictures. It was not the only way to make films (vide the avant-garde and silent-era montage), but Ferguson was convinced it was best. It respected both the medium and the way people lived.

Knowing How Everything Is Done

Ferguson's regard for trim, conscientious work fitted Hollywood's can-do approach to narrative. But he went beyond appreciation of the studios' unfussy storytelling to ask about the how behind the what.

James Agee declared at the start of his career that he didn't want to go behind the scenes of film production, fearing it would make him too forgiving. "My realization of the complexity of making any film would be so much clarified that I would be much warier than most critics can be in assigning credit or blame." By contrast, Ferguson seems to have thought that grasping the complexity of moviemaking could only enhance your appreciation of the artistry—while, admittedly, making you more merciful. He really wanted to know, with exactitude, how movies were made.

This impulse fits his critical credo. "Critics of all sorts are more often incompetent in the fundamentals of their own craft than not." In writing about jazz, he assigned the critic two tasks: "(1) to spread knowledge and appreciation of his subject among those who don't know but might learn about it; (2) to encourage those who are doing the work and tell them how it is 'coming over,' with as little bias and as much understanding as possible."

He goes on:

> And that is quite a task, requiring a constant and humble passion to know everything of what is being done and how everything is being done; and just as steady a passion for learning how to explain this so that it will somehow mean something to the performer and his audience alike. The best people I have discovered to learn about music from are actual musicians, who would not be found dead in the kind of talk used to describe their work.

What did Ferguson mean by knowing "everything of what is being done and how everything is being done"? The passage invokes the sort of insider skills he delighted in explaining in his jazz essays. By analogy, he expects the film critic to acquire some craft knowledge. The man who crouched close to the piano wanted to know as intimately as possible how the thing he loved came to be.

From April to June of 1941—what a time to pick—Ferguson was in Los Angeles. Editorial infighting at the *New Republic* "banished" him there, Cowley tells us, but Ferguson's explanation was more upbeat. "The paper is sending me to Hollywood to see if there is one." He filed interviews with the likes of Fritz Lang and Garson Kanin (both Ferguson favorites) and longish essays on the mores of the colony. He learned the iron grip of distribution, the venality and corruption behind the scenes, and the weary compromises, the cry we still hear today: "I made that one so I could make them give me this one." He also started to have hope for the future, noting the rise of director-writer pairings, the growth of independent production, and the increasing freedom allotted to filmmakers.

He kept reviewing. The year 1941 was one of Hollywood's greatest, and as ever Ferguson had the luxury of writing only about the films that interested him. Before he went west, those included *Kitty Foyle* (Ginger Rogers again), *Go West*, *High Sierra*, *The Lady Eve*, and *Meet John Doe*. In LA he saw *Penny Serenade*, *Citizen Kane*, *Man Hunt*, and *The Road to Zanzibar* ("the funniest thing I have seen in years. Years"). After his return to New York, he filled out his weekly assignment with essays about Hollywood and reviews of *How Green Was My Valley*, *Tom, Dick, and Harry* (Ginger again, in "the best-made picture of this year"), *The Little Foxes*, *Sergeant York*, *The Maltese Falcon*, *Never Give a Sucker an Even Break*, and *Dumbo* ("an endless wonder").

Through the 1930s Ferguson had kept an eye on the image, and sometimes he got quite specific. He noted how the camera twisted during a semisubjective sequence of *Private Worlds*, and he suggested an alternative method of directing a scene in *A Tale of Two Cities*. His stay in Hollywood seems to have sharpened his eye further. He focused, as we've seen, on the cadence of Bette Davis's walk in *The Little Foxes*, and he enjoyed the purely pictorial scenes in *Penny Serenade*.

For all the lack of action in the strictest sense, you will notice whole sections here where narration has been devised purely for the camera—which as the first and loveliest instrument in this whole orchestra is too often neglected. Frequently they do a whole scene without talk, and at one point they set up to catch the mood of a leavetaking from down the stairs and through the banisters, catching only the lower third of the full-length picture above.

3.2 *Penny Serenade* (1941).

His sensitivity to visual storytelling, along with his regard for directors like Stevens who "keep the mood clean and firm," led him to a harsh
verdict on *Citizen Kane*. He liked Welles's performance, the music, some
of the most striking shots and scenes, and "the recklessness of its inde-
pendence." The film was, he granted, a constant excitement to those who
loved the medium. But he also thought it episodic, talky, thematically
banal, ostentatious in technique, heavy with symbolism, and emotionally cold.

Ferguson's response was consistent with his sense of the Hollywood
aesthetic. The 1930s tradition was mostly light and fast. *Kane* was heavy
at some moments and accelerated at others, with abrupt transitions and
lines spasmodically interrupted by the start of the next scene. Although
the dialogue was fairly swift, there was little physical movement. Talk
ruled. "Kane is described, analyzed, asked about, remembered, talked into
existence and practically out of it." The good 1930s film flowed, but *Kane*
seemed clogged, with all its flashbacks and special effects and underlighting and floor shots and mirrored corridors.

A picture so bursting with bravado challenged Ferguson to get explicit
about artifice. The classic style aims, as film scholars would say decades
later, to be "invisible." It presents the story lucidly and without too
much flash. There can be playful moments with the camera, as in Ernst

Lubitsch, or montage sequences that are pretty fancy. But to be reminded of the camera or the cutting throughout the movie violated the premises of a style that put storytelling first. For Ferguson *Kane* was a return, in spirit and sometimes in substance, to the high jinks of Soviet montage and avant-garde film. The best technique served to "avoid monotony, hold the interest, and lead easily from one thing to another, *the devices for illusion being always and necessarily hidden in the natural emergence of the illusion itself.*" The italics are his.

The Camera Way

What caused *Kane*'s show-offishness? Ferguson was explicit: Welles hadn't made enough pictures. He didn't have practice at reconciling technique with emotional engagement, so instead of involving the viewer in the story, he asked for admiration of his audacity. His preciosity evaded the demands of craft, and by making each scene a showstopper he avoided the hard work of true continuity.

Just how hard that work could be was disclosed to Ferguson in two set visits he paid during his Los Angeles stay. In the 1930s he had outlined a rationale for the modern Hollywood movie. Now, at the beginning of the 1940s, he could go into the kitchen and see things whipped up.

Ferguson valued honest labor in any realm, and in Hollywood he found what he had always expected. Movie people worked very hard, six days a week from nine till six and beyond. Add to this the scale of the operation. On the set of Warners' *Out of the Fog* (at that point called *The Gentle People*) he stood before the life-size ship built for another picture, alongside the vast Warners tank and a dock running down to it. There he watched the endless maneuvering of lights—moved a foot this way or that, switched on or off, supplemented by spurts of fog fanned across the set. He saw James Wong Howe sitting calmly and calling out instructions "until every shadow has been painted in or erased or tinted to suit his precise liking."

Thomas Mitchell, Ida Lupino, and John Qualen rehearsed one shot, then played it out again and again. This was real work. The waiting—standing there for minutes offside, unable to move or talk for fear of spoiling a take—was as wearing as scrambling to pivot a light, thicken the air, or change a camera magazine. Once the shot was done, the actors' positions were marked and the next setup started to be prepared. We don't know about all this sweat when we see the ninety seconds or so it will consume on the screen. But Ferguson, a man who cherished his time watching swing bands rehearse, asks us to appreciate how even the most ephemeral shot demands "all the bewildering skill and loving care of miniaturists and watchmakers."

Ferguson's second set visit chronicled the filming of a scene in *The Little Foxes*. In a passage I've mentioned already, he expresses admiration for the small steps that take Bette Davis into an eye-locked exchange with Herbert Marshall on a staircase. Ferguson continues with an homage to the director, William Wyler.

> It is actually the man who devised this much, to put her in the center of the screen, to warn us in advance, to give us that sense of an even count up to the point of collision, and then, seven, eight, collision. And that man is the director; it is in a picture like this that you can see him at work.

Anticipating a polarity that would be made famous by French critics later in the 1940s, Ferguson tacitly compares Wyler's discretion with Welles's showmanship. He titled the Wyler piece "The Camera Way Is the Hard Way," an obvious rebuke to Welles. But during the set visit, Ferguson doesn't dwell on Wyler as an impresario. He has other ends in view.

The scene is a simple piece of exposition. Zan and the servant Addie are arriving in a carriage to have breakfast, and Zan's Aunt Birdie greets them from an upstairs window. Zan calls up to her and asks permission to skip the difficult part of a piano piece she'll play tonight. Birdie refuses to let Zan off and starts down to help the girl rehearse.

Again, Ferguson stresses the work involved. The morning on the set has been spent trying out some angles and dialogue lines, and the afternoon will be spent shooting the whole scene. Actors go through the entire action over and over as the camera, on a crane, is shifted among four positions. Shots are taken out of continuity, and many takes will be printed to make sure there are no flaws undetected during shooting. Throughout it all, the lights are adjusted, lines are spoken differently, and the number of takes climbs.

This account adds something to the report on *Out of the Fog*. Now Ferguson, watching the camera assume different angles, imagines how the final result will be cut together. To do this, he supplies an overhead diagram. He admits it's rough and incomplete, but as he discusses the camera setups and the action they capture, he shows an intuitive but fine-grained understanding of the stylistic choices characteristic of classical cinema.

October, 1941   5

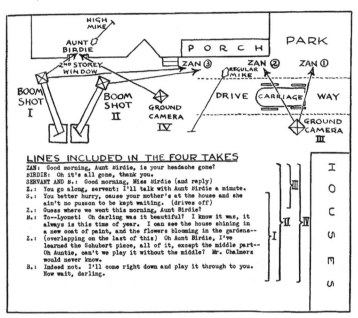

LINES INCLUDED IN THE FOUR TAKES

ZAN: Good morning, Aunt Birdie, is your headache gone?
BIRDIE: Oh it's all gone, thank you.
SERVANT AND B.: Good morning, Miss Birdie (and reply)
Z.:   You go along, servant; I'll talk with Aunt Birdie a minute.
S.:   You better hurry, cause your mother's at the house and she
        ain't no pusson to be kept waiting. (drives off)
Z.:   Guess where we went this morning, Aunt Birdie?
B.:   To--Lyonet! Oh darling was it beautiful? I know it was, it
        always is this time of year. I can see the house shining in
        a new coat of paint, and the flowers blooming in the gardens--
Z.:   (overlapping on the last of this) Oh Aunt Birdie, I've
        learned the Schubert piece, all of it, except the middle part--
        Oh Auntie, can't we play it without the middle? Mr. Chalmers
        would never know.
B.:   Indeed not. I'll come right down and play it through to you.
        Now wait, darling.

3.3 Diagram of camera setups in an early scene in *The Little Foxes*. From Otis Ferguson, "The Camera Way Is the Hard Way," *National Board of Review Magazine,* October 1941, 5.

Today, for example, we'd say that the establishing shot (fig. 3.4; more or less setup III) relies on a classic schema that uses OTS (over the shoulder) framings. Ferguson is more concerned with purpose. "The first thing is established: the audience must know where it is, who is talking to whom." He then imagines how Wyler will cut the ensuing dialogue, with Birdie at her window and Zan down below (figs. 3.5 and 3.6, setups IV and I). The camera setups put us midway between the two: we look up at Birdie and down at Zan, in a shot/reverse-shot situation. This string of shots will rely on what Ferguson claimed *Citizen Kane* neglected: cutting for reaction. "One of the first things in making a word effective is in showing its effect on someone—so after the cutting room has got through, we see Birdie as Zan is speaking to her, Zan as she hears Birdie." This is indeed what happens in the finished film.

By today's standards, Ferguson gives us only the first approximation of an analysis. Still, for possibly the first time in American film criticism, a reviewer describes a scene shot by shot in relation to production

3.4 The low-angle establishing shot.

3.5 The low angle on Birdie.

3.6 The reverse angle on Zan.

practices. In doing so, he not only stresses the intense labor that goes into the presentation; he also reminds us that we don't notice either the style or all the work that went into it.

Indeed, the very point of all that sweat and numbing repetition is to create a commonsense continuity. If we were in the scene we would look up at Birdie, as Zan does, and then look down on Zan from Birdie's vantage point. Hollywood's old adage, "Never let style distract from story" (still heard today), is clearly echoed in this passage, which stands in contrast to *Citizen Kane*'s flaunting of artifice:

> This business of repetition, changes, repetition, changes: you don't see it in the picture, but they were not just playing leapfrog. In fact, the very reason you don't see it is its own justification: you are not conscious of camera or effects, for the little bit flickers past in the final version and you are conscious only that a story is starting as you follow. Only!

Today some would consider Ferguson an apologist for Hollywood's sovereign control over our attention. In the 1960s and 1970s, film scholars grew suspicious of the invisible style, seeing it as a way of passing off specific ideological values as natural. For my part, I think it's a moderately stylized system. It's not wholly "natural," but like perspective in painting, classic continuity filming does capture some regularities of our everyday interaction with the real world. However you line up on this debate, though, we have to acknowledge that Ferguson pointed the way toward a deeper understanding of what Hollywood is doing.

Ferguson's death in his mid-thirties is one of the greatest losses American film culture has suffered. In his last year as critic and civilian, he began to explain, with a precision few had tried to attain, how this cinema created the qualities he had admired for years: flow and engagement, continuity and unity, the integration of detail with naturalistic storytelling. He could show his readers that even a bad movie is damned hard to make.

His 1942 farewell to criticism, insulting as it was to his peers, was burdened, I think, with a bitter regret. Now he was starting to understand the craft of movies from the inside, as he had with big band music. But at this moment he had to leave the field to people who couldn't care less about such things.

The movies were moving forward, but criticism wasn't. "May not the ship desert sinking rats?" As it happened, others would have to take up the task of understanding how simplicity and emotional force were born out of the most complex and expensive art on earth.

4 *James Agee*

ALL THERE AND PRIMED TO GO OFF

I guess I don't really like criticism, including my own.

JAMES AGEE, 1950

In 1944 a thirty-five-year-old man wrote about a fourteen-year-old girl he saw in a movie.

> She strikes me, however, if I may resort to conservative statement, as being rapturously beautiful. I think she also has a talent, of a sort, in the particular things she can turn on: which are most conspicuously a mock-pastoral kind of simplicity, and two or three speeds of semi-hysterical emotion, such as ecstasy, an odd sort of pre-specific erotic sentience, and the anguish of overstrained hope, imagination, and faith. . . . I think she and the picture are wonderful, and I hardly know or care whether she can act or not.

This review of *National Velvet* became one of James Agee's most notorious pieces. That wasn't because of the mash note creepiness we sense today, but because it encapsulated, almost parodically, a critical voice that still seems unique. The piece typifies his feverish emotionalism (*rapturously, ecstasy, anguish*), his back-and-fill qualification (*talent, of a sort*; *mock-pastoral*; *semi-hysterical*), his appeal to noble nouns (*simplicity, imagination, faith*), and not least his effort to capture the elusive tonalities of feeling. What is *overstrained hope*? What is *erotic sentience* when it's *pre-specific*? When did late-phase Henry James start writing movie reviews?

The passage earned a hearty raspberry from Theodore Strauss, who considered it typical of Agee's notion that a sentence was "the longest distance between two points." But that was a view from Los Angeles. Between 1942 and 1948, Agee's film reviews for the *Nation* and *Time* won him a cultish reputation in eastern provinces. He was lionized for his movie columns in a way he hadn't been for his poetry or his barely noticed book with Walker Evans, *Let Us Now Praise Famous Men* (1941).

Young people buzzed around him. To Alfred Kazin he personified brilliance. "He made everything in sight seem equally exciting. . . . He seemed at any time to be all there and primed to go off." Dwight Macdonald, an early friend and mentor, considered him "the most broadly gifted writer of my generation."

He exemplified the bohemian genius. He was addicted to cigarettes, booze, and philandering. He was unkempt, unbathed, and shabbily dressed. He refused to get his bad teeth fixed. Yet all was forgiven when he started to talk. He could raise a party to an exhilarating pitch, for hours. His hands writhed and snapped as the words poured out, and his voice held people rapt. John Huston wrote, "He is smiling. It stops raining all over the world."

Reviewing movies took him into filmmaking. When *Time* agreed to send him to Hollywood in 1944, he filed admiring reports on Selznick and other moguls. His impassioned defense of *Monsieur Verdoux* (1947) won him an acquaintance with Charles Chaplin, who nonetheless declined Agee's efforts to provide him a screenplay. His review of *The Treasure of the Sierra Madre* (1948) won a thank-you note from John Huston; their growing friendship led to Huston's invitation to write *The African Queen* (1951). By the time Agee died in 1955 he had stopped writing criticism, but two major screenplays, *African Queen* and *Night of the Hunter* (1955), carried his name. His most lasting literary fame came with the posthumous Pulitzer Prize novel *A Death in the Family* (1957) and the reissue of *Let Us Now Praise Famous Men* in 1960, which became relevant to the Other America debate about rural poverty.

The *National Velvet* review encapsulates Agee's style and critical sensibility. He's trying to embrace the whole Elizabeth Taylor experience, trying to convey in mere words the incandescence he finds in her. Instead of delivering a final, fixed judgment in a clever epigram, he shares with us his effort, pushing against the limits of language, always approximating, trying to capture shimmering outlines in a lightning sketch.

The task is that of the congenital Romantic, the artist who knows that every experience, every item in the world, flickers with obscure energies. These the artist tries to convey, usually in vain. The privileged vehicle for this nearly hopeless pursuit is lyric poetry, and Dwight Macdonald considered Agee at bottom a poet. Yet Macdonald also thought that Agee's greatest love, from the start, was movies.

In 1929, when he was twenty, Agee read Thomas Wolfe's *Look Homeward, Angel* and William Faulkner's *The Sound and the Fury*. Both sculpt southern literary and rhetorical traditions into self-conscious artistic shapes. I think he was obliged to face the question, What more is there for *me* to do? Part of his task, I submit, was to discover the possibilities of traditional Romantic expression in the young art of cinema.

On the Rough Wet Grass

When we consider any critic, a reader's first question is about personal taste. What did Agee like and dislike?

He admired films that had a documentary strain, or at least a realist one, though I'll try to nuance that judgment shortly. Agee entered the middlebrow-culture debate obliquely, often by castigating the "suffocating genteelism" that was creeping into Hollywood. He disapproved of prestige pictures like *Mission to Moscow*, *The White Cliffs of Dover*, and *Wilson*. He praised many foreign imports such as *Farrebique*, *Open City*, *Man's Fate*, and *Shoeshine* ("one of the most fully alive, fully rational films ever made"). Yet he was also suspicious of "pseudo-simple, sophisticated-earthy things from France." Like Otis Ferguson before him, he tried to keep watch on self-conscious artiness.

Like Ferguson as well, he regarded the director as the major creator of value in a film. He admired Howard Hawks, Preston Sturges, Alfred Hitchcock, Billy Wilder, Carol Reed, Raoul Walsh, Fritz Lang, and Vincente Minnelli. He was surprisingly indifferent to Orson Welles, though; *Citizen Kane* made him feel old. David O. Selznick wasn't a director, but Agee realized he might as well have been, so thoroughly did he control what appeared on the screen. He respected Selznick's understanding of American household routines, his ability to integrate weather conditions into his dramas, and his shrewd knowledge of what would move his audience.

Early in his reviewing career Agee deplored the shoddy quality of nearly all American studio pictures. He despaired that this art of potentially Shakespearean range was near to self-destruction. But he cheered up in 1947, noting several pictures of importance, and in 1950 he was positively ebullient: "Most of the really good popular art produced anywhere comes from Hollywood."

We might speculate that the 1944 trip to the West Coast showed him a new side of the films, as did Ferguson's stay in Los Angeles. Or perhaps his brightening prospects of working with Chaplin and Huston made him more optimistic. In any case, Agee had the sympathetic intellectual's hope that this new art's potential could be realized by people of talent, even occasionally genius.

We can talk about his likes and dislikes for a long time, but as with Ferguson, Farber, and Tyler, substantial ideas underlay his opinions. Central to Agee's perspective on cinema, I think, was a Romantic conception of art. As a person he seems to have tried to be every Romantic poet rolled into one. Drink (Poe), melancholy (Keats), womanizing (Shelley, Byron), thoughts of suicide (many of the above), consuming ambition laced with self-doubt and self-hatred (ditto)—these thread their way through his life. To round off the conventional pattern, he died young, felled by a heart attack at age forty-five.

Like most Romantics, Agee the artist sought a transcendent beauty in the ordinary world. Each moment, no matter how mundane, hums with a vitality that we can sometimes register, especially in childhood or at moments of calm contemplation. Science can't measure this burning core of life, but art can reveal it to us. The uniqueness of each thing, the streaks in a tulip or the wrinkles on a face, is to be noted, captured (however imperfectly), and treasured.

Not that we're stuck on the surface of things. The artist's imagination turns concrete reality into symbols—not schematic signs but rich, evocative images that throb with emotion. A Grecian urn, a deserted abbey, a chimney sweep: each becomes a dense cluster of impressions and implications, never shrinking to merely an abstract idea. Lyrical poetry, Wordsworth noted, is "the spontaneous overflow of powerful feelings." The poet tries to capture those elusive feelings, and ideally the poem presents that very struggle as its drama. Keats, writing of the nightingale that awakens him from a numbing stupor, tries to be at one with the bird in his imagination, at once delighting in the prospect and admitting its impossibility.

After publishing a book of verse, Agee carried his urgings into lyrical prose. The key example, and probably his most-read piece, is "Knoxville: Summer of 1915." As so often in his work and in Romantic writings, the child becomes the privileged point of access to experience, but the child's response is framed by adult awareness. "We are talking now of summer evenings in Knoxville Tennessee in the time that I lived there so successfully disguised to myself as a child."

The memoir starts with exact observation. We get the geography of the neighborhood, the habits of the neighbors, the characteristic activities of children and mothers and fathers. The fathers water their lawns, the gestures that regulate the hose ("in a compromise between distance and tenderness of spray") being described in considerable detail. Then come the dry rasp of the locusts and "the sweet cold silver noise three-noted" of the crickets. Soon the watering is done and families gather on their porches—talking, watching passersby, listening to the streetcar. The text bursts into one-sentence paragraphs, rendering nightfall as "one blue dew" alive with scents and sounds.

In the backyard, the family gathers on quilts, staring up at the stars. Abruptly the lyrical speaker is given a piercing glimpse of how transient this serenity is, and a prayer becomes an apostrophe.

> By some chance, here they are, all on this earth; and who shall ever tell the sorrow of being on this earth, lying on quilts, on the grass, in a summer evening, among the sounds of the night. May God bless my people, my uncle, my aunt, my mother, my good father, oh remember them kindly in their time of trouble; and in the hour of their taking away.
>
> After a little I am taken in and put to bed. Sleep, soft, smiling, draws me unto her: and those receive me, who quietly treat me, as one familiar and well-beloved in that home: but will not, oh, will not, not now, not ever; but will not ever tell me who I am.

A family's relaxation on a summer night has come to symbolize the pangs of mortality and identity, mixing love and fear into a childhood epiphany. Or perhaps the epiphany is constructed afterward, by an adult trying to put into words the exactness of a moment's memory and the yawning mystery that lies beyond.

Javelins, Transfixions

The struggle to expose the heart of reality without wounding it is dramatized more painfully in *Let Us Now Praise Famous Men*. In 1936 Agee and photographer Walker Evans were sent by *Fortune* magazine to report on the life of Alabama tenant farmers. After living there three weeks, the pair returned with probably the most famous documentation of poverty in American journalism. Agee's article, "Cotton Tenants: Three Families," was rejected by the magazine. The expanded version, with Evans's plain-spoken photographs, was eventually published by Houghton Mifflin in 1941 and received with general indifference.

American literature has its share of ungainly masterpieces, from *Moby-Dick* to *Gravity's Rainbow*, and *Let Us Now Praise Famous Men* joins their company. It oscillates with bewildering speed among description, meditation, and self-laceration. Declaring at the outset that this book won't ingratiate itself with any reader, Agee defies the conventions of reportage that had been consolidated in the 1930s. Historian William Stott has shown that *Let Us Now* tries to galvanize the reader into awareness by refusing all the clichés of Depression documentary: no dramatizing of scenes, no effort to report conversations verbatim, no comparing the tenants to animals or natural phenomena, no attempt to win readers' favor, and no call for simple reforms. Agee seems to start from the case-study model so common in the 1930s. But as the book unwinds, that form is abandoned because he wants to respect the absolute uniqueness of these people. Agee sacrifices typicality for singularity, and in the Romantic mode he sees in that singularity something universal.

It's one thing to recall a childhood evening on a middle-class Knoxville lawn. It's another for a Harvard-educated journalist to live with people whose washbasin is a hubcap and whose children sleep alongside rats gnawing the family's shoes. Why should a magazine aimed at the wealthy, staffed by reporters who will return to their comfortable lives, humiliate a harmless and helpless family? Agee's tone accordingly swings from lacerating confession to bitter irony: his book is "written for all those who have a soft place in their hearts for the laughter and tears inherent in poverty viewed at a distance."

Agee is torn in so many directions by the bad faith behind his assignment, and he records his agony in such painful terms, that the book becomes about a man suffering from hatred for himself, his place in the world, and his efforts to adjust his obscene job to the affection and respect he feels for the families. In sidewinding, often bewildering sentences, Agee tries to get beyond the awful good intentions of his project and to see the families and his disquiet both in concrete human terms and in cosmic dimensions. *Let Us Now Praise Famous Men* reads as if Faulkner's Quentin Compson had set aside his family obsessions and looked straight at the South he lived in.

Cotton Tenants, Agee's original version, was a compassionate but drily written account of the round of the families' lives. The last chapter ends with lapidary accounts of death.

> Invariably people work as long as they can stand up to it, and this
> is as much out of tradition and pride as of necessity and poverty.
> It is the same with death. Frank Tingle had seven uncles and every

one but one died with his shoes on, and that one had one shoe on and died trying to pull on the other one.

The book-length version expands the inventories and measurements of the households, the rooms and the possessions and decorations, as well as portraits of the families. As in the short version, Agee includes sexual confessions pertaining to erections and such, which alone might have been enough to spike the piece back in Manhattan.

The larger, deeply Romantic point is that facts, even close-up details, don't automatically deliver truth. Agee was insistent on art's moral dimension and the artist's duty to meditate on ultimate human concerns. The frustration of the *Fortune* assignment brings home to him that the most adequate account of these people's lives would consist of a galaxy of facts beyond comprehension.

> Here at the center is a creature: it would be our business to show how through every instant of every day of every year of his exis-tence alive he is from all sides streamed inward upon, bombarded, pierced, destroyed by that enormous sleeting of all objects forms and ghosts how great how small no matter, which surround and whom his senses take in as great and perfect and exact particularity as we can name them:
>
> This would be our business, to show them each thus transfixed as between the stars' trillions of javelins and of each the trans-fixions: but it is beyond my human power to do. The most I can do—the most I can hope to do—is to make a number of physical entities as plain and vivid as possible, and to make a few guesses, a few conjectures; and to leave to you much of the burden of real-izing in each of them what I have wanted to make clear of them as a whole: how each is itself; and how each is a shapener.

This declaration of purpose reads like something out of a preface; actually it comes well into the book. The young man who had admired Proust and Conrad must find a form for his experience. In place of the well-made novel of the early century—Henry James's tidy constructions, with lamps angled to light up aspects of a single subject—Agee offers a Whitmanesque, roiling swell that can't be reduced to geometrical archi-tecture. It's under revision as you read it, constantly restarting. A first part, listed in the contents but hard to find, gives way to a lengthy Book

Two that is a mixture of journal and scrapbook. There are appendixes (themselves collages); instead of being placed at the very back of the book, here they're followed by another section "(On the Porch: 3)" that, like the Knoxville memoir, ends with darkness, nature, and sleep.

The book even rehearses some of the possible ways of organizing itself. Addressing the families he has lived among, Agee writes,

> I might suggest, its structure should be globular: or should be eighteen or twenty intersected spheres, the interlockings of bubbles on the face of a stream; one of these globes is each of you.
>
> The heart, nerve, center of each of these, is an individual human life.

It's easy to mock the DIY indiscipline of this sprawl. But read in your youth, ideally late on a summer night, this roaring and whispering testament, accompanied by Evans's bone-hard imagery, can make you angry, sorrowful, and drunk with exhilaration. One of the first multimedia experiments, *Let Us Now Praise Famous Men*, Agee tells us, is "a *book* only by necessity." I think it's struggling to be a film.

Movies on the Page

Agee fell in love with film early. Opening sections of the autobiographical *A Death in the Family* show the boy Rufus (bearing Agee's middle name and nickname) coming out of a screening of Chaplin and William S. Hart movies. In the late 1920s, Agee was writing to Macdonald praising *The Last Laugh, Variety, Greed, Salvation Hunters*, and *The Battleship Potemkin*.

He drafted imaginary screenplays, two of which were published. *The House* (1937) and a sequence treating a portion of André Malraux's novel *Man's Fate* (1939) are exhaustingly virtuoso exercises in prose and film style. Both teem with fancy effects derived from late silent and early sound films, of the arty kind that Ferguson mocked. We get odd angles, fast motion, pulsating cutting, underlighting, looks to the camera, graphically matched dissolves, black frames with sound effects over, rhythmic synchronization of image movement with sound. Alexander Dovzhenko is one evident model, and Agee recommends that the cutting for *Man's Fate* be like that in *Arsenal*. When Agee and Farber planned a film in the 1940s, Farber pulled out: "He had so many Russian-type shots he scared me to death."

Agee's fussiness is astonishing. In the *Man's Fate* scenario, the resonance of a tolling bell is expected to match "the rhythm of the grain in the film, as if it produced the sound." Characters are seen reflected in bayonet blades. Descriptions of cuts and camera movements in *The House* go on endlessly and minutely. These texts suggest the world's hardest-working dilettante.

Remarkably, Agee's later Hollywood screenplays often contain the same minute instructions. Here is a comparatively brief instance from *The Blue Hotel.*

> The CAMERA is well toward the front of the room, height of the eyes of the seated men; Scully MEDIUM in r.s., players LONG, down center-to-left.
>
> Scully is half out of his chair at the start of the shot; he stands up fast, his paper floating, forgotten, to his feet making the only SOUND in the room. His spectacles fall from his nose as he gets up but, by a clutch, he saves them in mid-air; the hand grasping them is poised awkwardly near his shoulder. From the moment he is on his feet, a solid two seconds of frozen tableau: the Swede half crouching out of his chair, a huge fist (not shaking) in Johnnie's face; Johnnie still seated, looking steadily into the blazing orbs of his accuser. The Easterner, gripping the arms of his chair, sits very still and is very pale.
>
> After this 2-second paralysis . . .

Joseph Mankiewicz is said to have remarked that a director following Agee's screenplay would have nothing to do. "I think," Macdonald writes, "he never gave up the dream of becoming a director, of expressing himself with images and rhythm instead of making do at one remove with words."

Cinema attracted him, I think, because he saw it as a new vehicle for that Romantic vision of life that informed his verse, fiction, and reportage. For an artist in this tradition, all art aspires to the condition of poetry.

Illusions of Embodiment

The filmmaker's problem is the opposite of the poet's. The poet's words already lean toward the symbolic. Verbal tokens are very good at evoking concepts and emotions, but they are, as Macdonald mentions, "at one remove" from things. The writer's task, Agee claims, is "to continually bring words as near as he can to an illusion of embodiment." By contrast, thanks to photography, cinema delivers that illusion of embodiment automatically. The creative task therefore is to transcend realism, to retain respect for the way things are while showing the fire at the core of the world.

Georges Rouquier's *Farrebique* (1946), a documentary on the life of farmers, must have resonated strongly with Agee's time in Alabama, but he sees the film as more than mere recording. Rouquier

> realizes that, scrupulously handled, the camera can do what nothing else in the world can do: can record unaltered reality; and can be made also to perceive, record, and communicate, in full unaltered power, the peculiar kinds of poetic vitality which blaze in every real thing and which are in great degree, inevitably and properly, lost to every other kind of artist except the camera artist.

Naturally he was sympathetic to many of the combat documentaries, which had the power to capture moments of truth with a piercing immediacy. *With the Marines at Tarawa* (1944) contains such a moment. Marines troop back from battle, registering no jubilation at their victory.

> One gaunt man, his face drawn with sleeplessness and a sense of death, glances up. His eyes reveal both his lack of essential hostility and his profound, decent resentment of the camera's intrusion. Just as he leaves the picture he makes a face, as a father might make a face at a child. In his eyes, in his grimace, he looks into the eyes of every civilian and whatever face that civilian is capable of wearing in reply. And in the eyes of the camera, with that salute, he meets the eye of history.

As you'd expect, Agee was encouraged by the semidocumentary impulse that created films like *Call Northside 777* (1948). He collaborated on the independent documentaries *In the Street* and *The Quiet One* (both 1948). But Agee thought a worthwhile realism could be achieved in fiction films as well.

Just showing a real town instead of a back-lot set, or nonactors rather than stars, can endow a film with a greater measure of gravity. More profoundly, Agee notes that after years of laboring under a dead tradition of screen acting, some gifted writers, directors, and performers have begun to show how people behave. As Ferguson had noted, fiction films were starting to bring in realistic gestures and gaits and glances. Agee finds that Jean Vigo's flights of fantasy in *Zéro de Conduite* are tethered to exact observations of how schoolboys jostle one another and pantomime rebellion. Hitchcock is nobody's idea of a realist, but in *Notorious*, Cary Grant captures "the cultivated, clipped puzzled-idealist brutality" of a man Agee knows in a similar job. *Lifeboat*'s confinement to a tiny space is a gimmicky premise, but Hitchcock overcomes it by "an implacable physical and psychological realism." He squeezes "poetic and symbolic power" out of the situation.

Even on a sound stage the filmmaker can create a fictional world that is faithful to the textures of life, and the camera can capture that faithfulness "in the present tense"—that is, give it an immediacy that literature can't. But that mission demands that filmmakers learn to look steadily at the world. Makers of combat movies should study the documentaries for "the faces and postures and total image of actual warfare." Agee suggests that Wellman's *Story of G.I. Joe* (1945) has done that.

> It not only makes most of its fiction look like fact—and far more intimate and expressive fact than it is possible to record on the spot; it also, without ever inflating or even disturbing the factual quality, as Eisenstein used to, gives fact the constant power and meaning beyond its own which most documentors—and most imaginative artists as well—totally lack feeling for. I don't insist on the word if you feel it is misleading, but most of this film is good poetry, and some of it is great poetry, and all of its achievements, and even most of its failures, are earned in terms purely of moving pictures. The sudden close-up, for instance, of a soldier's loaded back, solidly intricate with the life-and-death implements of his trade, as he marches away from his dead captain, is as complete, moving, satisfying, and enduring as the finest lines of poetry I know.

Ferguson wanted insights; Agee demands epiphanies.

Accuracy, authenticity, vitality: these god-words, in Agee's columns, signify how film can achieve a balance between concrete and abstract, the illusion of embodiment and the ramifying emotional resonance of things. Film has come to fulfill Shelley's prophecy that poetry turns all things, no matter how base, to loveliness.

Saint James, and One of Two, Literally

Otis Ferguson wrote with great assurance. His prose suggests that he'd made up his mind when he sat down to write. Although metaphors or grammatical swoops might pull you up short, you knew where Otis stood. Agee, on the contrary, was famous for what looked like equivocation.

> *The Miracle of Morgan's Creek*, the new Preston Sturges film, seems to me funnier, more adventurous, more abundant, more intelligent, and more encouraging than anything that has been made in Hollywood for years. Yet the more I think of it, the less I esteem it. I have, then, both to praise and defend it, and to attack it.

I don't think you can stop reading after a lead like that. You not only want to know what the writer thinks, you want to know *him*—a man who enjoys a movie on the first pass, rethinks that experience, and concentrates his intelligence on both supporting and questioning first impressions. Instead of a settled judgment, we get criticism in process, the tug and shove of a mind considering the contesting appeals of a movie.

This opening is tactful compared with Agee's panegyric to Elizabeth Taylor. There he may seem to be gushing like a fan, except that the passage, with its hesitant self-interruptions, has that Agee blur of intoxication and the search for the exact word to embody it. A friend is sharing his excitement with you, in an apparently spontaneous burst.

The struggle enacted in the extended Agee review is double. He wants to do justice to the film and his experience of it; and he wants to convey, in the crosstalk of his sentences and paragraphs, the complicated act of judging anything. When the process seems too self-conscious, he can come off as a contortionist, resorting to the halt and stammer we saw in Stark Young. Writing like this, on *The Enchanted Cottage* (1945), makes you want to outlaw the comma and the concessive clause.

> As well as I could see, however, through fears generated chiefly by helpless rage against myself and my merciless assailant [the film], the movie was done quite well for the delicately vulgar sort of thing it is, especially by Robert Young and Dorothy McGuire. I can hardly imagine, for that matter, being seriously offended by Mr. Young; whatever he does, he is honest and sympathetic beyond offensiveness. Although I am happy to have to respect Miss McGuire's sen-

sitiveness and proficiency, I can't help feeling sorry to see her use such coarse, all but village-idiot bids for pity-please as the worst she uses to communicate the heroine in her humbler phase.

Macdonald observed that "Jim was always moderate in an immoderate way."

At times, however, one of his *Nation* reviews could squeeze his vacillations of judgment into the sort of verbal double takes we associate with Farber. On *Old Acquaintance*: "What perplexes me is that I could sit through it with some interest." A pure Agee opener, this on *Open City*: "Recently I saw a motion picture so much worth talking about that I am still unable to review it."

Another level of vacillation: trying to be true to your feelings, but also being aware of how those can be manipulated. Agee realizes that he is vulnerable to the soft side of Hollywood; he realizes that the intelligentsia will pounce upon hokum and bathos. Yet he realizes that hokum and bathos sometimes slip into genuine emotion. Consider one of the biggest tearjerkers of the period.

The *Hollywood Reporter* called *The Human Comedy* (1943) "the best picture this reviewer has ever seen," and *Variety* declared, "This is one of the screen's immortals." A family that has already lost its father may lose its eldest son in the war, and there is nothing the members can do but keep steadily moving through routine days in their small town. Much of the action centers on a telegraph office through which most war news comes, and that news is mostly about boys who won't be coming back. The telegraph operator is sinking into alcoholism, and the delivery boy, working nights to help his family, learns about quiet human suffering.

The Human Comedy invites us to patronize it. Its sentimentality makes it hard for today's sophisticated cinephiles to enjoy without guilt. Ten minutes into it, you get a lump in your throat, and you may feel like a sucker. It hits us below the belt again and again. Accordingly, Farber, the toughest guy in the back room, faces *The Human Comedy* as a hanging judge.

For *Time* Agee reviewed William Saroyan's original novel, and addressing that readership he is largely sympathetic. He praises certain scenes as subtly lyrical, presented "in words of almost primer lucidity." Perhaps the pathos of boys growing up without their father, and the naïveté of boys who can't read wandering in awe through the town library, aroused Agee's own memories. He deplores the novel's absence of any recognition of evil or of moral complexity, but he leaves the reader admiring Saroyan's "chronic ecstasy, an almost Franciscan loving kindness and optimism."

Reviewing the film for the *Nation* he is, no surprise, more conflicted.

> Most of my friends detest it. A good many millions of other people, I suspect, will like it . . . I do not agree with either side. I think my friends are too frightened of tearjerkers to grant that they can be not only valid but great, and that the audience at large is too friendly, too gullible, too eager to be seduced.

He labels Saroyan a "schmalz-artist," but that's a characteristically mixed call. Agee praises his affection for little people while objecting to his mawkishness. In the finished film, Agee finds truth glowing out from details, like the soft clink of horseshoes at dusk or the scene ("full of death and enigma") of three servicemen roistering off to war on a rainy night. He praises the casting of a young nonactor as the child Ulysses, whose scenes yield "something perfectly limpid, true, warm, and powerful."

Yet there is so much slickness in the movie, so much condescension and ignorance of human behavior, that Agee grows furious. He draws up a list of missed opportunities, centering on a good idea—riders in a train coach join in song—that is spoiled by "the overswift, disgraceful 'informality' of a musical-comedy chorus." By the end of the review he is near despair. "Why did they bother to make the film at all? Why, for that matter, do they bother to make any?" Deeply moved by the possibilities glimpsed in the film, he is far more scathing here than in his routine dismissal of ordinary product.

His efforts to be fair to both the picture and the very act of judgment, his windiness and his concision—these qualities take on poignancy when you realize how compulsively Agee worked. At *Fortune*, he always overwrote and finished little of what he started. Macdonald, also hostage to *Fortune*, jotted a note in 1935: "No interest in his work here and small ability for faking. He spends three times as long on his pieces as he should, and he has a devil of a time with them." Agee's work areas were jammed with papers, magazines, clippings, ashtrays, and memorabilia, with whiskey and Benzedrine on hand. His abandoned projects filled grocery cartons.

According to his biographer Laurence Bergreen, Agee enjoyed writing for the *Nation* and was usually on deadline. But turning out ephemeral notices for *Time* seemed to have been torture. Writing in longhand, he composed as if he were Proust. When Ezra Goodman took over the reviewing post, he made a discovery that was "blood-chilling." He found over thirty rewritten versions of the opening paragraph of an Agee review, often with only a word or punctuation mark changed.

Long-form prose invited him to exfoliate, as he had with *Let Us Now Praise Famous Men*. The novel *A Death in the Family* was unfinished when he died. On his mass-market think pieces, Agee chronically missed deadlines. He thought he could write his appreciative essay "Comedy's Greatest Era" in a few weeks; it took him a year.

Still, I think journalism kept him comparatively on target. Writing to deadline and format channeled Agee's volcanic energies. On his screenwriting jobs he seems to have been conscientious. Even then, though, he couldn't do anything by halves. On the *African Queen* script he wrote through the night, after a day of tennis, talk, and drink with Huston. The ordeal, wholly self-inflicted, contributed to his first heart attack. It seems he couldn't go long without writing.

Agee's frank subjectivity in the *Nation* pieces yielded a bracing sense of an actual person talking to you. Instead of supplying a fixed assessment, he dramatized the act of wrestling out a provisional sense of the film's accomplishment. After seeing four or five films a week, sometimes revisiting certain ones, he would labor through a piece that tried to sum up everything. All the while, his rhetoric projected an exquisite sensibility trying to do justice to each film at hand, to his immediate experience of it, and to that experience as recollected in (relative) tranquillity.

As the years went by, he became somewhat more analytical and objective, aiming for more precise description of what was happening on the screen. He was always shot-conscious, and he was sensitive to actors' performances, but the short *Nation* reviews usually render very general judgments. In reviews devoted to a single picture, he can quicken details, like the soldier's backpack in *G.I. Joe*, so that the generalities (poetry, dignity, human divinity) get some ballast. Often he needs annoyance to rouse his attention, as in the *Human Comedy* review. He protests the arty stylization of *The Ox-Bow Incident* by pointing to the "phonily gnarled lynching tree" and the sound of "angelic soprani" whenever a black preacher appears.

One of his descriptive strategies, which Ferguson had occasionally tried, involves redirecting the movie. Objecting to a particular handling in a film under review, he provides a new script. He suggests some better ways to shoot and cut scenes in *For Whom the Bell Tolls*, and he wishes Rouquier had used infrared film and stop-motion for night scenes in *Farrebique*.

He's especially hard on the evasive treatment of drunkenness in *The*

Lost Weekend. What has Wilder missed? The causes of Birnam's alcoholism, the many moods of drunkenness, the chronic narcissism, self-
loathing, and self-pity, and the "horrible distortions of time" suffered in
a hangover. Agee couldn't speak with authority about movies treating
military strategy, but the whole spectrum of drunken sensation was vivid
for him, and ripe for poetic transmutation.

> Sound and light peculiarities could have been impacted in the
> film and track by appropriate, dry exaggeration. A knocking radia-
> tor, an abrupt auto horn, coupled with the right kind of playing,
> might have told the audience as much in an instant as an hour of
> pure objectivity could. The light equivalents of flashing traffic on a
> sunny autumn day, as Birnam might experience them, might drive
> an audience moaning from the theatre, unless their exact realism
> were modified into art.

We are back with the literary scenarios of the 1930s, mental movies
stamped onto the page with forbidding specificity.

Lady-Killer

It's possible that Agee's increasing attention to a movie's look and sound
owes something to the influence of his friend and fellow critic Manny
Farber, but just as important was the impact of two filmmakers. Each
teased him into the sort of sustained scrutiny that countered critics of
mass culture by paying close attention to how a film worked.

Agee considered Charles Chaplin a genius. He felt on seeing *Modern
Times* "as if Beethoven were living now and had completed another symphony." Agee began reviewing after *The Great Dictator* (1940) had come
and gone, so his principal encounter with Chaplin's new work was with
Monsieur Verdoux: A Comedy of Murders (1947). He devoted three *Nation*
installments to it, an unprecedented gesture for him. He uses the space
to show in detail how film artistry can create the sort of dense symbolic
statement we find in poetry and drama. In short, he interprets the movie.

Monsieur Verdoux tells of a discharged bank clerk who, in order to keep
his wife and child secure in their country villa, seduces women and murders them for their money. He shuttles from city to country, Paris to the
provinces, juggling affairs and assuming different guises—an antique
dealer, a sea captain, a construction engineer, a bon vivant. Verdoux
eludes the police only to lose his wife and son in the early 1930s. He's

recognized by the family of one of his victims and is arrested, convicted, and hanged. On his way to the gallows, he is serene, even smug, claiming he is simply conforming to the world he lives in. Murder is business, and he just operated on too small a scale. "Wars, conflict—all business. . . . Numbers sanctify."

Verdoux abandoned the lovable Tramp character, begged sympathy for an insouciant killer, and seemed to confirm Chaplin's public persona as a skirt chaser and Communist sympathizer. The mainstream press mostly hated the film, calling it too preachy and lacking in comedy, but some venues, including the *New York Times* and left-leaning magazines, praised it. After a largely hostile press conference, at which Agee defended Chaplin, *Monsieur Verdoux* was withdrawn. A new publicity campaign failed to ignite public interest, and the film became the biggest debacle of Chaplin's career so far.

The first part of Agee's review defends "this great poet and his great poem" by answering critics who declare the film unfunny, immoral, tasteless, poorly cast, talky, and creakily old-fashioned in its direction. His rejoinders rest on the assumption that Chaplin is parodying clichés, not recycling them. The apparently casual compositions are a "mock formlessness" that have an integral beauty, as in the garden wedding reception. The churning train wheels depicting Verdoux's commuting are a well-worn transitional device, but by repeating the image so often, Chaplin makes it funnier each time, while suggesting Verdoux's growing desperation. And there are some visual jokes harking back to silent tradition, such as the ridiculously distant shot showing the rowboat from which Verdoux plans to jettison Annabella.

Agee advances his interpretation in the review's second installment. The irony of Chaplin's story is that Verdoux is a model of the responsible paterfamilias, seeking to provide for his family after he's fired from his bank job. You can take him as standing for the businessman or the warmonger, but Agee suggests that at bottom he displays the split personality that society forces on any modern man. His wife and child represent the good in him, his cycle of murders represents the evil. To protect the good he must "exercise all the worst that is in him." As the film proceeds, his idyllic private life becomes an illusion that serves only to justify his crimes.

Compartmentalized, as we would say, Verdoux's life is poisoned not only by the killings he commits but by his secrecy. At home he's playing a role no less deceptive than his masquerades for his victims. The frozen bliss of the household grows ever more perfunctory. The wife, saying she would have been happy to be poor, becomes sad and passive. In locking up wife and child in "a shrine and a jail," Verdoux destroys the happiness they all might have had. Meanwhile, Agee asserts, Verdoux grows correspondingly monstrous, loving his family's helplessness and savoring "his true marriage, which is to murder. . . . He is the loneliest character I know of."

Agee's last column on the film considers the denouement. There are some mysteries here. Why does Verdoux say he "lost" his family? According to Agee, this is symbolically vague: his loved ones died through "segregation and deceit." Why does he turn from the Girl, now a rich man's mistress in a limousine? Because long before this, he spared her life, and this one moment of weakness, granting affection to a person outside the family circle, rebuked his single-minded effort to split his life.

Most critics took Verdoux's suave courtroom and death-house epigrams as Chaplin's own critique of modern society. Agee, though, reads for irony. He sees Verdoux's banter as more posturing, another masquerade. Verdoux is still asserting "his dream of himself," his illusion that what he's done can be justified. Lacking his original domestic pretext for murder, all he can do is shift the blame from himself to society. The Tramp, a quasi-divinity, has been replaced by a deeply secular bourgeois, the essential "upright man" who refuses to face all he has done. Verdoux's wit as he strolls to the gallows is the final touch of the film's characteristically brisk and cold "savage gaiety."

I think Agee's ambitious attempt to trace filigreed meaning in a film owes something to his training. After courses with I. A. Richards, dean of England's "New Criticism," the young Agee felt "a clear, tingling daze." He came to maturity when New Criticism was gaining a foothold in American academe and the literary and political quarterlies. By the late forties, thematic interpretation based on close technical analysis, usually demonstrating some deep ambiguity or irony within a lyrical voice, was emerging as the dominant strain of literary criticism.

A 1940s movie reviewer didn't have opportunities to examine films as closely as a scholar could pick apart a poem. Still, some intellectuals made a start at comparable "deep reading." Eric Bentley contributed an inspired essay comparing *Verdoux* to Pirandello's plays, while Parker Tyler pursued more wayward but equally enticing paths. Perhaps Agee's imaginary screenplays are a sort of displacement of New Critical scrutiny: microscopic dissection he can't exercise on an actual film gets enacted with a virtual one.

In any event, the *Monsieur Verdoux* columns show that when engaged by an artist he adored, Agee could be a remarkable close reader of films. His essay suggests that a film needs to be examined patiently, with all the resources of imagination and sympathy that F. R. Leavis or William Empson brought to literature. Farber called Agee "a fine antidote to the paralyzing plot-sociologists who hit the jackpot during the 1940's." In one sustained burst, Agee rebutted the critics of mass culture who simply did not know how to watch a movie.

A Man's Man

The *Verdoux* review-essays showed that Agee could brilliantly interpret plot and character. Given the teeming details in Agee's screenplays, you'd expect him to dig into the style of the films as well. We've seen that he does sometimes mention a close-up or a sound effect, particularly in documentaries, and he's quite attuned to actors' behavior. On the whole, though, he seldom strives, as Ferguson and Farber do, to convey the visual texture of a movie.

An exception is his profile of John Huston. Agee started writing too late to review *The Maltese Falcon* (1941), and he didn't review the two other releases Huston signed before leaving for the war (*In This Our Life* and *Across the Pacific*, both 1942). But he admired "the sullenly beautiful documentary *Report from the Aleutians* [1943] and the magnificent *San Pietro* [1945]." He picked Huston's *Let There Be Light*, a controversial and eventually suppressed documentary about soldiers recovering from battle trauma, as one of the best pictures of 1946. Primed and ready to go off, Agee wrote after the 1948 release of *The Treasure of the Sierra Madre* that Huston was, "next only to Chaplin, the most talented man working in American pictures."

He sold *Life* on the idea of a profile, and delivered it in 1950, two years later than promised. He grew close to Huston, and in September of 1950 they began work on the screenplay for *The African Queen*. Agee's first heart attack, suffered during his stay with the director, put him in the hospital, but he continued to contribute to the screenplay, which was finished by Huston and the uncredited Peter Viertel. Despite some attempts, Agee didn't work with Huston again.

The *Life* piece is part celebrity profile and part appreciative essay. Much is made of Huston's roustabout adventures in boxing, the Mexican cavalry, and the battle in *San Pietro*. Agee, like Farber, prefers his movies and moviemakers "virile." Yet Huston is also an intellectual, reading Joyce, Hemingway, and O'Neill in his spare time. He paints, hunts, shoots, breeds horses, and loves to gamble. The image is of a robust, risk-loving artist at home with both action and ideas.

Agee had some reservations about the director's work, but it took Huston to rouse him to the sort of exactitude of perception on display in "Knoxville," *Let Us Now Praise Famous Men*, and his essay on silent comedy. The Huston piece was almost the last significant film criticism he published, apart from an alert, typically conflicted assessment of *Sunset Boulevard* published later in 1950.

For Agee, Huston's films embody a vital professionalism. Huston's style is immediate, smooth (*pace* Ferguson), and mostly invisible. It stays, as modern critics would say, in the moment. Yet it can blossom into the sort of poetic implications revered by the Romantic. In *We Were Strangers* (1949), a student is gunned down at Havana University.

> A scene follows which is breath-taking in its surprise and beauty, but storytelling, not beauty, brings it: what seems to be hundreds of young men and women, all in summery whites, throw themselves flat on the marble stairs in a wavelike motion as graceful as the sudden close swooping of so many doves. The shot is already off the screen before one can realize its full meaning. By their trained, quiet unison in falling, these students are used to this. They expect it any average morning. And that suffices, with great efficiency, to suggest the Cuban tyranny.

Like a good poet, Huston discovers both meaning and beauty in the uniqueness of his material, not by imposing abstract ideas. On the set, he offers his performers only a few hints, letting them find their characters themselves. He suggested that the Mexican bandits in *Sierra Madre* surround Bogart but stay close to the ground. The result is jittery and fateful, capped by one bandit's slither to Bogart's feet in a movement "as innocent as a child's and as frightening as a centipede's."

Huston's style is versatile, sometimes simply letting the camera run and sometimes using aggressive traveling shots. In close-ups, he huddles characters' heads to pack the frame; long shots relax the tension. Agee treats *Sierra Madre* as Huston's most fully achieved film, where the camera stays in the middle distance and the "clean" and "tight" presentation yields compositions that are well designed yet seem informal (figs. 4.1 and 4.2). Later films are more ostentatious, but each achieves an individual style: sweltering physical confinement to the hotel in *Key Largo* (1948) and harsh lighting contrasts in *We Were Strangers* (figs. 4.3 and 4.4).

4.1 *The Treasure of the Sierra Madre* (1948).

4.2 *The Treasure of the Sierra Madre* (1948).

4.3 *Key Largo* (1948).

4.4 *We Were Strangers* (1949).

At the same moment that Bazin was speaking of Wyler as a director who gave viewers freedom about where to look, Agee celebrates Huston's ability to arouse the eye. In his comments on one composition in *Sierra Madre* (fig. 2.1), he shows that the story action of checking Cody's pockets continues while the framing supplies a portrait of each man. The casually packed composition inspires Agee to propose, perhaps for the first time, the now familiar notion of the active viewer. "Huston is one of the few movie artists who, without thinking twice about it, honors his audience. His pictures are not acts of seduction or of benign enslavement but of liberation, and they require, of anyone who enjoys them, the responsibilities of liberty."

Henceforth, the idea of the shot as an open field of information, leaving the spectator to assess what's important, will be part of the critic's tool kit. It extends the Ferguson legacy by showing how behavioral details of individual men in a group can be compressed into a single shot. This is, I think, what Agee thinks a poet with a camera can do.

It's terribly easy to be sentimental about Agee and almost as easy to be hard on him. But I think that reading him can do something rare in film criticism: he calls you to act on your best instincts. His dithering can be frustrating, and he often snaps open too many pipes in the sonorous organ of that style. Nonetheless, he teaches us to look, listen, and feel more sensitively. As Parker Tyler put it in 1944, the viewer's obligation is *"to see as much as he can take away with him."* Now, seventy years later, Agee can still help us do our job.

5 *Manny Farber*

SPACE MAN

Emanuel Farber is today's star among my Rhapsodes. He is the cinephiles' favorite, and his tastes, his ideas, and his prose have had enormous influence. The Library of America collection of his writings comes festooned with praise from Martin Scorsese, Richard Schickel, Richard Corliss, and William Gibson. "The liveliest, smartest, most original film critic this country ever produced," asserted Susan Sontag.

Farber carried the controlled ecstasy of the 1940s critics into later years. A 1969 essay on Howard Hawks describes *His Girl Friday*:

> Besides the dynamic, highly assertive pace, this *Front Page* remake with Rosalind Russell playing Pat O'Brien's role is a tour de force of choreographed action: bravado posturings with body, lucid Cubistic composing with natty lapels and hat brims, as well as a very stylized discourse of short replies based on the idea of topping, outmaneuvering the other person with wit, cynicism, and verbal bravado.

The outpouring of words, the piling up of adjectives and modifying phrases, the ellipsis (no time to spare for *ands*, let alone periods), and the sideswipe reference to modern painting all bear the signature of a critic who knows how to make enthusiasm infectious. Even the repetition of *bravado* within the same sentence, which looks like an amateur boner, rings with its own—well, bravado.

He's no less adept at the honorable American craft of grousing. Where Agee gave us elegant, if sometimes tormented, efforts to be fair to all, Farber can act utterly fed up. A 1957 essay picks Larry Rivers, Dave Brubeck, and *Twelve Angry Men* as examples of the new middlebrow confidence man.

> The figure who is engineering this middle-class blitz has the drive, patience, conceit, and daring to become a successful nonconforming artist without having the talent or idealism for rebellious crea-

tion. The brains behind his creativity are those of a high-powered salesman using empty tricks and skills to push an item for which he has no feeling or belief. Avant-gardism has fallen into the hands of the businessman-artist.

Farber's career breaks, almost too neatly, into distinct periods. From early 1942 through 1946, he reviewed films for the *New Republic* and published art criticism there and elsewhere. Then he stopped writing for over two years. In early 1949 he signed on at the *Nation*, taking over after James Agee left. He covered film and some visual art until January 1954. For other venues he wrote longer pieces, many of them now famous. After another hiatus from 1954 to 1957, he resumed writing film criticism, often with Patricia Patterson, before stopping altogether in 1977.

His best-known work comes from the early fifties, when he celebrated B-level crime films and hard-guy studio directors (Hawks, Walsh, Fuller, Siegel). He coined labels like "underground film" and "termite art" to describe his B film poets, while Hollywood's straining significance could only seem "white elephant art." His late phase brought his dense appreciations of Jean-Luc Godard, Rainer Fassbinder, Michael Snow, and other contemporary filmmakers, as well as extended essays revisiting action directors of the classic era.

The dominant image of Farber's tastes didn't arise by accident. When he compiled his essay collection *Negative Space* (1971), he included only two pieces from the 1940s proper and a few from 1950. His essays "The Gimp" (1952) and "Underground Films" (1957) set the tone and framework for the book. In "John Huston" he created a piece out of 1949 and 1950 reviews and recast it in keeping with his later thinking.

The writing he selected for *Negative Space* reinforces another aspect of Farber's image: the aesthete cowboy. Farber had played football and baseball in high school, and instead of turning his painting skills to commercial illustration, he became a carpenter, a trade that sustained him for decades. He seems to have been at home in the pugilistic Abstract Expressionist circles of the 1950s. Clement Greenberg claims to have bested Farber in a fistfight, although Farber scared him. ("He could have beaten me up. . . . He had big hands.") Years later Andrew Sarris reported that during a critics' meeting Farber nearly clobbered John Simon.

In print, Farber punched at all weight levels and liked to work in close. He said that Agee "paid out tribute like a public-address system." He called Sarris "a boneless Soupy Sales," and he found Susan Sontag "cat-like" and possessed of "a confidence that her knowledge is all-purpose (if contracted, she'd show up in Vietnam)." The man who admired tough noirs declared Rock Hudson a mama's boy and confessed, "I don't understand the belt people get out of overwrought feminine pictures."

Negative Space remains such a dazzling collection that we've tended to neglect Farber's earliest years. It's there that we find his ties to the emerging critical tradition I've been charting. For a little while, then, let's pretend that Late Manny never happened. No worries about being disappointed: his writing is from the start racy and engaging. Moreover, by rummaging in his youthful art reviews, we can get a better sense of exactly what his criticism owes to the visual arts. The result isn't quite what we might expect.

Color Commentary

Farber had trained at art schools in California before he married another art student, Janet Terrace. After living for a while with Farber's brother in Washington, DC, the couple moved to Greenwich Village. In January 1942 Farber started reviewing art for the *New Republic*, and soon he took Ferguson's film beat as well. "Ferguson went off patriotically to war in the Merchant Marine and died. The next day I was asking for a job as movie critic. I was never very sentimental in that period. I was ambitious."

At age twenty-five Farber found himself in competition with two of the most formidable figures on the cultural scene. Clement Greenberg and James Agee were only eight years older than Farber, but they had a big head start. They overshadowed him at the time and for decades afterward.

When Greenberg started reviewing painting and sculpture for *Partisan Review* in 1940, he was already famous. He had published two major essays in the journal, then the bible of the progressive literati. "Avant-Garde and Kitsch" (1939) had kicked off the mass culture debate that would surge through the next two decades. Showing the same knack for sharp-edged synthesis, Greenberg's 1940 essay "For a New Laocöon" made a strident case for abstract art as the culmination of ambitious Western painting.

Greenberg asserted that painting had for centuries been dominated by other arts, notably literature. Modern art had revealed painting's unique conditions of existence. From Courbet and the Impressionists to Cézanne and the cubists, painters had come to recognize that painting's power lay not in telling stories ("illustration") or portraying the world as photography could capture it ("illusion"). At last the painter, secure in knowledge of "the opacity of the medium," could create new visual experiences solely through line, color, and form. Purism was now the painter's mission.

Greenberg benefited from a vacuum in America's popular and elite press. Although abstract art was widely accepted in Europe, most American critics were hostile. Many major magazines had no art critics on their rosters. Academic art historians mostly focused on distant eras, and journalists either ignored or mocked abstraction and the other major movement of the period, Surrealism.

Greenberg, an amateur painter, had no scholarly training in art. Most of what he had to say was old news to painters and scholars in the modernist camp. He derived most of his ideas about technique from lectures by the influential émigré Hans Hofmann. Still, Greenberg told a good story, and he treated modern art as initiating a new epoch in the history of visual expression. The progress of painting, loosely tied to changes in social structure, led inevitably to the defiant austerity of abstraction.

As a subtle reader, brilliant polemicist, and shrewd packager, Greenberg managed to get the intelligentsia excited about one major wing of new art. The readership of *Partisan Review* numbered only about eight thousand, but they were the right eight thousand. In late 1942, Greenberg expanded his campaign to the pages of the *Nation*. There, as the magazine's first art critic, he ceaselessly promoted "the direction in which the pictorial art of our times must go in order to be great." By the end of the decade, the painters Greenberg came to champion—Pollock, de Kooning, and a few others—would be recognized as modern masters, and he would be hailed as a prophet.

Farber's views were partly in harmony with Greenberg's. Like most critics, he took abstract art and Surrealism to be the primary trends of the moment, and he valued the emerging Abstract Expressionists highly. He saw problems with "illustration," especially that as melodramatic as Thomas Hart Benton's. He could talk about picture planes and integrity of materials with the best of them. But his criteria were pluralistic and his analytical categories surprisingly traditional.

Contra Greenberg, Farber discusses pictures in relation to their subjects as well as their techniques. He analyzes compositions with art-school finesse, pointing up triangular designs and strategic symmetries. He doesn't concentrate wholly on abstract art, and he respects representational masters like Max Weber and Utrillo (in a startlingly extravagant review). Above all, Farber values feeling. Where Greenberg asks if a painting falls into step with the march toward purism, Farber looks for emotional expression.

In several passages we can read a covert dialogue with Greenberg. Snippets from Farber's 1942 reviews add up to a manifesto pleading for the importance of emotion—that of the artist and that of the viewer.

> The really important part of the painting—the feeling that the artist wanted.

> The essential function of painting [is] the honest individual emotion put down forthrightly without too much regard to the weight of centuries of painting already done, and conventions already explored.

> The artist is supposed to react emotionally to his environment in color and line, if his audience is ever to.

> Weber always pushes a gesture, a stance, or simple area of color to its fullest emotional presence. There is never any doubt of what you feel from any spot in his canvas.

> [Tchelitchew] manages to convey his gloom no matter how badly he paints. . . . There's a place for a wider scope of emotion in painting, and this Russian artist shows how moving and universal extreme introspection can be in painting.

> I have yet to see a painting which reminds me of [picture] planes, and I'm sure that Rousseau wasn't feeling planes when he painted tigers.

By 1945, Farber has become perfectly explicit. "The purist argument inevitably starts by narrowing painting down to a matter of designed line and color on a flat surface instead of showing that design is constantly driven, controlled, and ordered by the expression."

Art criticism had always sought a balance between analysis of the painter's craft and a consideration of how the craft conveyed meaning and feeling. In the finished work all these factors give evidence of the artist's personality. Farber's adherence to this traditional view didn't block him from appreciating new art. It simply allowed him to treat all art as potentially exciting.

In order to appraise how well artists achieved expressive form, Farber mobilized his gifts as a writer. Like Ferguson describing swing, he made pictorial technique come alive. In a Fletcher Martin picture "a horse tosses a cowboy sky high, but the painting is done with ease and no weight thrown around. The wise handling of rhythmic line and feathery color is enough for this artist to get across the action." As for Goya,

> When his pictures were allegorical, Goya moved from naturalism to supernaturalism, to goats, donkey-people, chinchilla rats, and the witches and brownies (nice witches), and in either approach there is the definite human imprint, the unmistakeable [*sic*] earmark of man. It is a matter of detail, of his driving deeper and harder into the idiosyncratic detail, so that it is realized at its most knobby, crooked, or bent likeness.

And, not for nothing, there is sheer representational skill: "Goya could draw a bull out of this world."

But when an overblown concept created chaotic form, as with Benton's war series "Year of Peril," Farber called foul.

> His painting now is apt to be Jesus on the cross, being harpooned from the ground by fascist goons and from the air by the light of a Messerschmidt. . . . There are a dozen different dominant colors in this painting and no relationship between any of them. They cross each other out. The conception is one of disunity since each form is dissociated from the others in the picture.

In German, a *Farber* is a dyemaster, and Farber lived up to his name in being especially sensitive to color. Greenberg famously misunderstood Mondrian's theories and ascribed to *New York Boogie Woogie* colors it didn't have. By contrast, Farber licks his lips when he talks of Chagall's lemon suns and raspberry patches of ice. The "testicle-like fruit" in a painting glows like gold velvet. Farber often notes "color rhythms," the ways a single hue varies in shade. In one painting Milton Avery expands "the vividness of the main color—the St. Patrick's Day green of the wall—by a scaled off series of dulled, almost dried greens." When an artist fails at color, as most watercolorists do, Farber calls the results anemic "for both pictorial and emotional reasons."

Eyedropper Aesthetics

Greenberg, unyielding foe of mass culture, denigrated certain painters as "comic-strippers." But if like Farber you're looking for feeling in art, why

5.1 Stan MacGovern, *Silly Milly*. From *trans/formation* 1, no. 2 (1951): 96.

not try the comics? After all, cartoons are designed to elicit a laugh. If they're really good, they're not relying just on dialogue or captions; they have to be drawn funny. As Agee trained New Critical close-reading tactics on *Monsieur Verdoux*, Farber brought traditional art-historical methods to the most vulgar form of popular imagery of his day. Whatever hints of academe those methods might have carried are stripped off by a lithe, vernacular style.

His virtuoso 1944 column on comics displays a connoisseur's delight. He notes that comics' golden age has given way to mediocrity, but he praises Ernie Bushmiller's *Nancy* (with its characters bearing "identical fire-plug shapes, two-foot heights, inch-long names"), *The Bungles Family* (with their memorable noses), and the now-forgotten *Silly Milly*.

> Silly Milly is drawn in typical McGovern style, as though by a wind current, and has a prehistoric animal for a hair-do, a very expressive, giant-size eye, and a perfectly oval profile. It is one of those comics with animated décor, like "Smoky Stover," with adjoining family portraits shaking hands, and one that tries for laughs in every part of the box. . . . It is one of the most sophisticated of comics, smart-alecky, corny, sloppy and half unlikable, but produces its eyedropper of humor each day, without fail.

Another form of popular illustration is practiced by the Mexican artist José Guadalupe Posada. Clement Greenberg called him limited in talent but fairly skillful, chiefly because he sensed the power of black and white "as sheer color." Farber, the practiced artist, explains the starkness of Posada's design as partly necessitated by scale (his bigger pictures are "the size of a slice of bread") and method (cutting in type metal leads to "closed, mean forms" and "staccato movement"). Farber doesn't forget subject matter either, offering a casual inventory of Posada's lurid scenes.

He was especially interested in showing executions and murders, which he depicted at the moment when the murderer's knife was on its way through the victim's throat, or just as the firing squad had emptied their guns. But he also leaned heavily on fires, collisions, accidental deaths, and he did two good illustrations of what the end of the world might look like.

Lyonel Feininger was one of the few serious painters who practiced comic-strip art, and perhaps that knowledge led Greenberg to dismiss him in a few lines. In the same amount of space, Farber conjures up the unique Feininger look.

A make-believe world like that of a little boy's fairy story, with its scratch-lined, bug-like people, scalloped bridges, Toonerville trains, streets and houses like those in the movie "Dr. Caligari," four-masted schooners (than which there are none more wondrous) in candy green seas under the inevitable yellow moon like a child's scissor cutout of the letter C.

In exactitude Farber outstrips Greenberg. Whenever the two reviewed the same shows and books, comparison favors Farber's pointed, funny analyses. Greenberg predictably issues gaseous generalizations and stern pronouncements about the inevitable future of painting or, more ominously, the eventual doom awaiting the painter he's reviewing. Consider the two men's handling of William Steig's morose little book *The Lonely Ones*. Steig was later renowned as a cartoonist and author of children's stories, but in the mid-1940s he was making a reputation as a satiric artist along the lines of Saul Steinberg.

Greenberg takes Steig's drawings as capturing the way modern people use personal confession as a weapon. They admit their loneliness but also seek pity in a self-aggrandizing way. Although Greenberg praises Steig for conveying ideas sharply, he concludes that what Steig gives us are cartoons, and thus "not quite art." His drawings rely on stereotyped imagery and don't meet modernist criteria. Line "is not felt for its own sake"; everything is given in comic-strip symbols, like raised eyebrows for surprise. Accordingly, Greenberg doesn't bother to analyze Steig's technique.

Farber drills deeper. He diagnoses Steig's first book, about neurosis, as less disturbing than this new volume, which teeters toward psychosis. Farber grants that Steig sometimes falls back on comics technique,

5.2 *Nerves* (William Steig). From Manny Farber, "Chaim Gross, Milton Avery, and William Steig," *Magazine of Art* 36 (January 1943): 15.

but in his best work his line has expressive qualities. It "defines sharply and cold-bloodedly the very crux of a crushing moment, the core of a disturbed personality." Even when he's not portraying people, his work is shot through with anxiety.

There could hardly be a more unpromising picture than figure 5.2. But Farber explains:

> In the rendition of *Nerves* (a ball balancing precariously on the edge of a table) perspective, tilt of the table, light and line all contribute to the fact that the ball will surely fall off, but when? In this particular drawing it is interesting to notice the details, which are so few and so unobtrusive as to go usually unnoticed—the conception of the unnaturally shaped shadow under the table is highly erratic and sprawling in contour, recalling the loose, watery, uncoordinated state of the nervous breakdown. This is in contrast to the sharp, ordered, concrete world of the table. Steig shows you the eerie, unsubstantial level to which the ball is about to plunge. The drawing of the table is equally interesting, because it carries, despite its unswerving realism, the feeling of the underprivileged little people that infuses everything that Steig draws.

You won't find, I think, anything as fine-grained in Greenberg's 1940s reviews. Farber the practicing artist finds emotional qualities in what Greenberg discusses, vaguely, as style and concept. Farber agrees that Steig's line isn't "felt for its own sake"; it's felt for feeling's sake. If he can get this much out of this simple drawing, you can imagine what he can do with Paul Cézanne, Piet Mondrian, and Robert Motherwell.

Farber's unpretentious emphasis on feeling as carried by form allowed him to do what the other Rhapsodes managed in their own fashion: to sidestep the mass culture debate and face popular art straightforwardly. And on occasion to embrace it. Farber's blunt acceptance of images, high or low, on their own terms is given great force by his style, a world away from the inflations of Greenberg and the obiter dicta of the *Partisan Review* cohort. Farber's colorful commentary—form plus feeling, scrutiny of detail, combustible diction—would become even more stirring when he moved to film reviewing.

The Ferguson Legacy

The other major figure confronting the young Farber was James Agee. After Agee's death, Farber would write about him rather brusquely, praising him but also calling him a thoroughgoing middlebrow, "a fall guy," a master of "verbal stunting," and a purveyor of "arrogant, omnipotent decisions." At the time, however, Farber appreciated his rival's stature. Despite the failure of *Let Us Now Praise Famous Men*, Agee commanded a following in New York literary culture. Farber became friends with him and they socialized frequently. During Agee's life, Farber seems never to have mentioned him in print, although Agee occasionally mentioned the younger man and arranged for Farber to become his successor at the *Nation*. "He made sure I got the job and I made sure I lost it."

In print, the two men's personalities were at odds. Agee's reviews were sensitive and eloquent, anxious and introspective. The earnestness extended the persona that dominated *Let Us Now Praise Famous Men*. Farber constructed a different persona: the straight-shooting, hard-hitting, cultivated roughneck. Yet both could be playful, and both were pledged to the Ferguson aesthetic. We find them accepting, for instance, Ferguson's general antipathy to arty pictures, talky pictures, "theatrical" pictures. They subscribed to his dictum that a good film flowed. It harnessed image and sound to the clear, vivid presentation of the story.

Echoing Hollywood's own aesthetic, Ferguson insisted that the audience shouldn't notice the artistry. "Its main problem always is story, story,

story—or, How can we do it to them so they don't know beforehand it's being done?" The result was an appreciation of the skillful subordination of technique. As he put it in his *Kane* review, the creation of the illusion is "hidden in the natural emergence of the illusion itself."

This straight, clean storytelling is endorsed by Agee, though he favors purely poetic epiphanies. Ferguson's imprint was deeper on Farber. His later work paid homage to Ferguson frequently, and without his usual acidity. Farber's classic 1952 piece "The Gimp" takes ideas and phrases from Ferguson's review of *Citizen Kane* ten years earlier. As late as 1977 he was referring to "what Ferguson wrote about the iron fence in *Citizen Kane*," as if every reader would have known that long-forgotten passage.

Pushing Ferguson's idea of invisible style to a new level, Farber notes:

> If the events are arranged to progress as though there were no camera present, if the camera merely watches and records what those events look like, the movie is to my mind the true nature of a movie; that is it is non-theatrical. . . . The actions and procedures of the event will be seen propelled solely by factors within the event itself, irrespective of the camera.

A good director, says Farber, is always "seeking the idea in the visual world of action and movement, which is the more suitable, and so more emotionally vital, manner for the movies." Like Agee, Farber held that this quality had been achieved during the silent era; both critics held up Griffith, Chaplin, and the rest of the silent-film canon as the sort of thing that sound cinema would have to match.

Farber had more at stake than did Agee and Ferguson. The demand for invisible illusion and narrative continuity clashed with the version of modernism that dominated the gallery scene. Greenberg and his followers declared that advanced painters would explore anti-illusionistic devices like surface values and spatial contradictions. Storytelling was best left to middlebrows like Norman Rockwell, who had mastered all the tricks of Victorian narrative painting. Modern painting, Greenberg thundered, should not illustrate. But according to Ferguson and Farber, a movie was at its core an illustration—a story told in action, by means of cinematic technique, made smooth and vivacious and emotionally absorbing.

The Style Is the Manny

I think what I set out to do with criticism in the Forties . . . was to set out the movie before the reader's eye in as much completeness as I could, in that topography. I had to develop a picture which could pull the audience in and give them these sights without their realizing it, and which would divulge the landscape of the film as accurately as I could get it. That involved a lot of color work in the language and in the insights—color work in the sense of decorative quality.

MANNY FARBER, 1977

At the level of writing, Ferguson had set the bar high. Here he is on *The Philadelphia Story*:

> Having expended so much care to such effect, [the filmmakers] might have considered also that it is only brooks in poems that go on forever without somebody's beginning to yawn, scratch, and wonder seriously whether it is the suspense or just his underwear that is climbing. . . . They could, I suppose have extended the very funny business at the expense of *Timelife* and its prose-bearing oracular baby-talk—though I wonder whether even the keen edge that is present as it is cuts any of the dull butter that must be out there haw-hawing at the performance and trundling up with a ring in its nose to the same newsstand afterward. . . . But there is nothing served in figuring out how to do something after someone has very well proved that it's done already because he did it.

This is tough to beat. Yet across the 1940s, Farber raises Ferguson's demotic prose a couple of notches in intensity. For example, masculine values (physical work, comradeship) are central to Ferguson, and both Agee and Farber use "virility" as a term of high praise. Characteristically Farber ups the ante, calling Maya Deren's films "lesbianish" and warning us against their "pansyish composing and lighting."

Farber's inflation of critical rhetoric is most evident when he ransacks the resources of figurative language. Usually it's recruited for ridicule, but it can add cracked humor to anything.

> Hyperbole: *Juke Girl* is "the most belligerent thing you've ever seen." *None but the Lonely Heart* is "one of the biggest hodgepodges Holly-wood ever constructed." Val Lewton is "the least commercial film

maker in Hollywood by about a hundred miles." *Murder My Sweet* is "by all all odds the most incomprehensible movie in years."

Metaphor: The protagonist of *Open City* "reminds you of a wet string." Bing Crosby "chews gum with jet-propelled jaws."

Comic personification: Hitchcock "impregnates costume and décor with so much crackling luster, so much tension and latent evil, that the spectator expects a stair corner or tie clasp to start murdering everyone in sight."

Comic understatement: The hero of *The Razor's Edge* is "deeply distressed by his war experiences." The hero's office in *A Rage in Heaven* is "rather stunted. . . . couldn't house more than eight or nine trains."

Comic overstatement: Ann Blyth is "about eighty years too young for what she is doing." The home in *Since You Went Away* contains "several hundred photographs" of the absent father. In *We Were Strangers* "the tunnel dug in a week by six proletarian heroes is the size of the Holland Tunnel."

Burlesque (Gertrude Stein department): "But most of all this picture was not very good and was made by MGM and that clinches the argument."

Paradox: *The Postman Always Rings Twice* "is almost too terrible to walk out of."

Then there's his gift for *paraprosdokian*, the sentence with a surprise ending. Ferguson was a master of the anticlimactic shrug, but Farber goes further. The most famous example is "*Stalag 17* is a crude, cliché-ridden glimpse of a Nazi prison camp that I hated to see end." Here's another: "The attempt seems to be to give the sensation of reading the book rather than looking at a movie, and I think it succeeds to a certain extent, anyway sufficiently to paralyze the movie."

One of Farber's most robust rhetorical strategies involves personal pronouns. Agee's paragraphs are studded with *I*'s as he reenacts the squirming push and pull of arriving at his judgments. Farber, who never plays out the hesitating agonies of appraisal, seldom resorts to *I*. He is a man for *you*. So is Ferguson, but he is often using it to address the reader directly. Farber employs *you* for the British *one*. In *The Big Sleep* "you try to decide what motivates the people." For *Open City*: "No one opens his mouth or takes a step without reminding you of dozens of other movies." Farber's review of *North Star* is a cascade of *you*'s, creating a reader who is simultaneously following his prose and watching a virtual movie.

The strategy is shrewd. When the critic's impressions are transferred to the hypothetical viewer (you), you're already halfway to agreeing with him. Moreover, the reader is flattered, especially when the critic attributes to *you* a knowledge of dozens of other movies. This just-pals mind meld asserts authority while implying equality. Pauline Kael lived off this device. I flinch every time I remember her claim that after seeing *Roxanne* (1987) "You want to go to the town; you want to go back to the movie."

Forms and Feelings

Farber's rhetorical maneuvers are often aimed at sharpening the sort of detail we find in his art criticism. In a short review, the critic must fasten on moments. These are typically faults or beauties, and perhaps they quietly signal how attentive the critic's eye is. Both Agee and Farber followed Ferguson in looking for vitality, honesty, and well-managed storytelling. Agee went further, seeking in the privileged moments a glimpse of transporting beauty. Farber, no Romantic, looked in cinema for the expressive significance he prized in painting.

So in *Casablanca* he's fascinated by Peter Lorre "wrinkling and unwrinkling his forehead faster than ever" or Humphrey Bogart, who "seems to be holding back a mouthful of blood." *The Glass Key* lets us dwell on the way a character "fondles a bottle he is about to crack over a skull." Farber mocks implausible neatness, as when five people enter a crowded movie house and conveniently get seats together. By contrast, *Youth Runs Wild* plays out "the whole visual vocabulary of a group like [Lewton's] high-school kids: their stance and gestures playing handball, smoking." Fresh details are best when casually caught, not studiously inserted. Laboring over striking effects would hurt the sense of action moving along without special concessions to the camera.

Just as we get more concrete evidence in Farber's art reviews than in Greenberg's, we get more of it in his film reviews than in Agee's. For Agee, *Counter-Attack* (1945) is something of a stunt. The movie confines itself mostly to a chiaroscuro-drenched cellar in which two Soviet partisans try to guard seven German soldiers while a battle rages above them. It isn't really hard, Agee says, to keep a movie alive in a confined space. He praises and criticizes the film in generalities: some formulaic defects, some virtues.

Farber devotes a long column to *Counter-Attack*, and he too has some objections, typically phrased more pungently than Agee's. Agee: Paul Muni is "too often an over-generalized, stagy embodiment of Russia." Farber: Muni's acting "is in a heavy, emphatic style that could be studied in detail from any distance up to a mile." The important difference, though, is that Farber soaks us in minutiae.

We learn that the Nazis are seldom seen in close-up or from within their group; that movements away from the group are "given grandeur" by the lighting and a building tension about exactly how far Muni will let an enemy walk toward him; that Muni delivers his orders like a whip crack; and that the film makes "the magician's performance of magic a hypnotic, dance-like affair with an insinuating pattern of sound supplied to identify the noise cigarettes make hitting the inside of a helmet as the magician throws them."

Farber's reviews take notice of current trends in theme, form, and style. He is exceptionally sensitive to the portrayal of African Americans in movies and never misses a chance to observe how even earnest problem pictures abridge black characters' identities. His brother was a psychiatrist, so he can spray mordant humor on the vogue for psychoanalytic mysteries: the doctor goads the patient into "recalling his one trauma—straining like a man lifting the Woolworth building."

He notices the vogue for flashbacks (though he usually dislikes them), the emerging conventions of war pictures, and the various roles ascribed to the hero. Farber salutes the clever opening of Preston Sturges's *Palm Beach Story* as an experiment, a "miniature movie" left hanging until the film's final shot. One funny essay on the prospect of Hollywood dada targets a host of clichés: tears welling up, entire meals finished after we've seen people eat only a few bites, cigarettes smoked down in a couple of puffs, notes immaculately handwritten in fast motion. What the critics of mass culture saw as mindless formula, Farber treats as a familiar joy in conventions that do neat work and seem silly only when you stop to think about them.

Farber fills out Ferguson's dicta by echoing the idea that movies express feelings. He worries that Sturges's films aren't "emotionally evocative," and he praises the lovers' kiss in *The Clock* as "one of the most awesome and emotionally accurate scenes in years." Even a weak film like *Rage in*

Heaven can be redeemed by the spasms of fear in Robert Montgomery's performance. *The Dark Mirror* gains its emotional truth in a remarkably visual way: the differences among the three main characters are underscored by each one's style of kissing. As with the paintings that Farber prizes, a movie excels when it presents feelings briskly, without leaden emphasis.

Negative Space, 2-D and 3-D

Is this all? Isn't Farber's main contribution to the critical conversation his expertise as an artist and a critic of modern painting? The 1940s criticism has fewer references to painting than we're used to in the later work. But he does, rather tentatively, start to consider movies pictorially. What's striking about his angle of approach, though, is that he treats cinema as *different* from modern painting.

Farber assumes that images are central to artistry in the film medium. But although his painting reviews often emphasize the geometry of pictorial composition, in reviewing films he's less explicit about this. He's chiefly concerned with the way the filmmaker captures the event expressively. In *The Stranger*, Welles creates excitement with moments that are "shot at an angle that gives you the hardest impact of the action." Tay Garnett's *The Cross of Lorraine* presents combat "with striking pictorial truth, complexity and force. He is always forcing the emotion of an action by getting the clearest, most direct views of it, by cutting his film so that the action continually strikes out at the audience."

Most films, Farber maintains, aim at a bland sheen but not at purposeful images. When a film is weak, "there is nothing in the people, costuming or acting that will intrigue your eye enough to keep it focused on the story." *Heaven Can Wait* is content to set the camera far from its actors and center them squarely and at eye level. *Lost Boundaries*, despite a laudable message about black Americans, is pictorially "as spineless as vanilla pudding."

> The photographer's head evidently comes off if he tries anything but the orthodox, group-portrait composition: central details a little above screen center, neither close to nor far from the camera.

What would the young Farber have made of Wes Anderson?

For Farber, the most memorable images carry the story's idea through both framing and staging: the political meeting in *The 39 Steps*, a scene in *The Ox-Bow Incident* with cowboys studying a painting over the bar. *Mr. Lucky* exploits "the position of a person in relation to his environment and the people occupying it with him." Farber goes on at length about how the scenes in a War Relief office jammed with people and partitions combines "architecture, pantomime and movie devices . . . with almost acrobatic invention." He invokes the idea of medium specificity as well. The whole sequence "uses all the components of a fluid medium, and the effect is a real movie one, neither theatrical nor literary."

This fluidity was crucial for Ferguson too, but Farber realizes it runs athwart the modernist demands about focused composition and the role of the frame edge. "Having a voice, eyes and legs, [film] is more fluid than any other medium. Like the mind, it is physically unbounded and can paint." It paints, he implies, not a Mondrian or a Malevich, in which the frame edges create their own dynamic, but something like what we find on an unrolling picture scroll. James Wong Howe's shots in *Air Force* reveal a space "uncentered in the old sense taken from painting, so that it seems to spread out in all directions past the boundaries of the screen." Anticipating Bazin's conception of the porous frame, Farber finds the unboundedness of cinematic space central to its power.

Accordingly, cinematic space that is too exactly composed seems overbearing, designed to be appreciated. Many 1940s films display tight composition with deep perspectives. But perspective was under suspicion in Manhattan's gallery scene. According to Hans Hofmann and other theorists, composition by line (e.g., linear perspective) was less forceful than composition by planes and masses. With these resources, the painter can build up volume through "negative space."

The term became a buzzword in the art world of the 1940s, having been emphasized in Hofmann's lectures and given explicit definition in Erle Loran's *Cézanne's Composition* (1943). For Loran, positive space consists of the masses in the depicted scene. Negative space amounts to the relations in depth among the masses (fig. 5.3). These spaces should be felt as forces, creating a three-dimensional "push-and-pull," as Hofmann called it. Accompanying negative 3-D space are negative *shapes*, which are the unfilled, jigsaw-puzzle portions of the composition.

Farber would use the term "negative space" broadly and metaphorically in later years, but he explicitly invokes negative space in the narrow sense in 1953, in relation to the enhanced depth of stereoscopic cinema. When 3-D films frame the shot through a horse's legs or wagon wheels, they create "a sort of hole" between the front plane and more distant ones, and the result is "a more exact impression of masses."

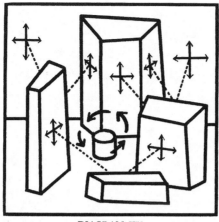

DIAGRAM XV

5.3 "The dotted tension lines indicate the amount of negative space that exists between the positive volumes." From Erle Loran, *Cézanne's Composition* (Berkeley: University of California Press, 1943), 43.

Farber applies the idea of negative space a bit more thoroughly earlier, in an important 1946 comment on William Dieterle's *The Searching Wind*. It's not a film Farber especially likes, but it does provide something quite different from the "stiff, contrived shot" that Welles favors. I believe he's objecting to Welles's habit of filling every inch of the frame, including hanging a big head in the foreground (figs. 5.4 and 5.5).

We speak of images like these as deep, but instead of summoning up negative space through tensions between the masses, Welles gives us something closer to a collage. The low angle of the Wellesian shot makes the three-dimensional relations *less* concrete; different-size figures and faces seem pasted into the frame. There's less a sense of varying *distance* (3-D negative space) than of varying *size* (2-D placement). There's less of negative *shape* as well, since every inch of the frame seems stuffed with points of interest.

Farber asks us to contrast *The Searching Wind*. That film's compositions have "the dispersed look of real life" (figs. 5.6 and 5.7). We get a natural-istic array of figures, and we grasp the axes of tension seen in Loran's diagram. The people have room to breathe, with well-articulated negative shapes of varying sizes spacing them out. They gain as well the volume proper to distinct compositional masses. "Garmes' photography," Farber adds, "makes the people seem bulky."

He goes on to another important point. A *Searching Wind* shot "gives you the feeling that you're in the room where the action is taking place."

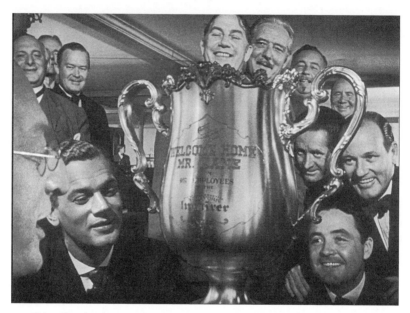

5.4 *Citizen Kane* (1941).

5.5 *The Magnificent Ambersons* (1942).

5.6 *The Searching Wind* (1946).

To the naturalism of spatial arrangement is added a sense of our presence. We look at the scene in a plausibly offhand way. But a Welles composition makes sense only when seen from a single vantage point; the shot is designed around our eye. Shift the camera a little to left or right in my Welles illustrations, and the composition collapses: people block one another. Shift the *Searching Wind* camera and the action would still cohere pictorially. This is, I think, what Farber suggests when he claims a scene can be presented in a way that suggests it would unfold with the same force if the camera had not captured it.

In sum, Farber accepted that it was legitimate for some contemporary painting to insist on the picture plane, to refuse illustration and illusion, and to recognize the active role of the frame edges. But at this point in his career he saw cinema as bound up with lucid storytelling. That demands an art that hides art.

Farber had a stronger pictorial sensibility than either Agee or Tyler. His gifted eye sized up cinema's visual possibilities. But he didn't see those possibilities as akin to modernist painting. Cinema was a new medium of pictorial artistry, with its own demands—demands for story, illusion, emotional arousal, indefinite boundaries, loosely composed figures—all those pictorial considerations that the Manhattan gallery scene found

5.7 *The Searching Wind* (1946).

suspect. Cinema was at its best when it blended authenticity and feeling with vivid but subtle visual form. Hollywood cinema, a popular art, could flourish through expressive naturalism.

The Movies Go Modern

Farber left the *New Republic* in 1946 when Henry Wallace, having been fired from Truman's cabinet, became editor. He returned to film reviewing in 1949 with a column in the *Nation*. This phase of Farber's career deserves detailed appreciation of its own, but I just want to indicate how it displays a sharp shift in his aesthetic and in his attitude toward what happened in the 1940s.

During those years, many American filmmakers began to stage and shoot their scenes in pronounced depth. If *Kane* did not start the trend, it provided a vivid demonstration. Very soon after its release many 1941 films—*The Maltese Falcon, Kings Row, The Little Foxes, Ball of Fire*, and others—displayed big foregrounds, steep diagonals, and several planes of action in more or less sharp focus. These techniques became salient features of black-and-white Hollywood dramas, and many color ones, well into the 1960s.

Yet almost no American critics of the time spotted this trend. Welles's technical innovations were well covered in the press, and most reviews of *Kane* mentioned what Gregg Toland had done, but reviewers didn't seem to notice other filmmakers' take-up of the style throughout the decade. Even Farber's *New Republic* pieces refer to depth staging in the oblique ways I've just mentioned, and he doesn't go into lens length, film stocks, lighting, and other matters that were widely discussed in the technical journals of the day.

By the early 1950s, however, Farber registered how the Hollywood style he had celebrated had changed. Not only were movies becoming more middlebrow, with prestigious projects trying to bring back the audience. Not only were acting styles becoming more extroverted, even neurotic. Movies were also becoming more stylistically aggressive—more, in a way, like modern art.

> 1950: American film-makers have suddenly learned how to make movies work as plastically as Mondrian paintings, using bizarre means and gaucherie.

> 1950: Directors, by flattening the screen, discarding framing and centered action, and looming the importance of actors—have made the movie come out and hit the audience with almost personal savagery.

It sounds odd to say that the deep-focus style of the early 1950s yields flat and shallow images. But the big foregrounds and background figures squeezed into a locked-in frame seemed to Farber a legacy of Welles's "stiff" shots. Directors were abandoning the spacious, dispersed framings of *The Searching Wind* and other films. Those films balanced figures and landscape while creating solid masses and expressive tensions in the negative space.

The spatial exaggerations of recent films brought home to him a stylistic change that had been gathering force for years. In 1952 he offers two somewhat different historical accounts. From one angle, he suggests there was a lag in picking up the excesses of *Citizen Kane*. He claims that Welles's film initially made little impact on veteran directors. Only now, with *A Streetcar Named Desire*, *A Place in the Sun*, *People Will Talk*, and other overbearing movies has "straight storytelling" lost out to shallow perspectives, "low intimate views," rigid staging, and plenty of faces in our faces—"huge, florid, eccentric, and somewhat sinister."

From another angle, Farber suggests that the decay wasn't delayed but was already setting in at the start of the 1940s. Some filmmakers embraced the fluid and open style. Val Lewton, for instance, always respected the balance between his characters and the scenery. So did Walsh and Hawks, who at their best conveyed "the truth of American life and the excitement of American movement." (Again Farber echoes Ferguson, who pledged Hollywood cinema to "the truth of life and the excitement of movement.")

But, Farber insists, early 1940s Hollywood also played host to Times Square intellectuals fed on left-wing theater and fiction. Their films pushed symbolism, political criticism, and fragmentary form. In this version of history, Welles isn't the only culprit; there are Sturges (*The Great McGinty*) and Kanin (*A Man to Remember*) as well. All displayed "very close, snarling presentation which put the actors practically in a nose-to-nose relationship with the movie spectator." It all led to William Wyler's *Carrie* (1952) with its shallow space, "the actors arranged parallel-fashion and statically on the front pane of the scene." Paradoxical as it may sound, American cinema decayed when it achieved the pictorial flatness Greenberg prized in painting.

Years later, in the introduction to *Negative Space*, Farber would add a few data points to these little histories, looking backward to *What Price Glory?* (1927) and its "illustrational" style, "scaled in human terms for the space of the screen." *The Big Sleep* (1946) is more compact and parsimonious in its coordinates, but it's still worlds away from *Touch of Evil*'s "disorienting, illogical, allegorical" space.

In the 1950s, in Farber's view, American movies had become worse than ever. There were, of course, the exceptions with which his taste became identified. After mildly advocating for B films during the 1940s, Farber now found them preferable to bloated prestige pictures. *White Tower* (1950), *Union Station* (1951), and *Kansas City Confidential* (1952) maintained "present-tense realism through low-budgeted, off-the-cuff, on-location technique." Later he would look back at the masters of the studio action picture and discuss them in the painterly terms—for example, *His Girl Friday*'s cubistic lapels and hat brims—that would dominate his writing in later years.

Manny and the Man

Farber's 1950s denunciation of recent trends made for contradictions he didn't confront. In 1943 he had praised *Kane* highly, finding it a challenge to the "visual sterility" of most Hollywood films: it made each scene "a vigorous new visual experience." There's no mention of Welles as a Times Square leftist intellectual. Similarly, in 1945 *The Story of G.I. Joe* had carried its point with "real cinematic strength," but in 1957 Farber considered it flat, sentimental, and merely a MoMA classic. In 1943 he had greeted Hitchcock as "producing movies of high quality," but eight years later the director became the master of "cheap, glossy, mechanically perfect shocks."

Sometimes the turnabout is startling. Upon release in 1946, *The Best Years of Our Lives* earned the most consistent praise Farber lavished on any film of the decade. It was "far and away the least sentimental, most human of current films . . . an extremely sensitive and poignant study of life like your own." A decade later, however, it became "a horse-drawn truckload of liberal schmaltz," one of those "solemn goiters" that get by because "they bear the label of ART in every inch of their reelage." Critics can of course change their minds, but they ought to acknowledge that they've done so. It's disconcerting when the critic castigates his fellows for inflating reputations that he pumped up as well.

Looking back at Farber's comments on John Huston, we find him declaring that "*The Maltese Falcon* is a good story which director John Huston told brilliantly on the screen" (1942). *San Pietro* has "breathtaking reality, fullness of detail and sharp effect from shot to shot" (1945). Yet by the time Farber returned to reviewing in 1949 he found Huston wanting.

Agee, as we've seen, found in Huston a rare level of excellence. His review of *The Treasure of the Sierra Madre* (1948) is in the Ferguson spirit:

There is not a shot-for-shot's-sake in the picture, or one too prepared-looking, or dwelt on too long. The camera is always where it ought to be, never imposes on or exploits or over-dramatizes its subject, never for an instant shoves beauty or special meaning at you. . . . His style is practically invisible as well as practically universal in its possible good uses; it is the most virile movie style I know of; and it is the purest style in contemporary movies, here or abroad.

It seems likely that Agee's praise for *Sierra Madre* triggered Farber's demolition of Huston. Farber was between jobs when the film was released (1948), but soon after he was hired at the *Nation*, he seized on *We Were Strangers* (1949) as an occasion to dismantle the career of "Hollywood's fair-haired boy." He redoubled his assault when *The Asphalt Jungle* (1950) was released.

Taken together, Farber's pieces set out to refute Agee point for point. According to Farber, Huston's characters are oversimplified, the stories are moralizing, and his vision of life comes down to the futile quest for money. Far from having an invisible style, Huston has an aggressive one. "The texture of a Panama hat is emphasized to the point where you feel Huston is trying to stamp its price tag on your retina."

Farber revisits a leitmotif of his early work, the idea that the best Hollywood cinema rested on the "unbroken action sequence" that presents a balance of figures and environment. The classic filmmaker viewed life "from a comfortable vantage point, one that is so unobtrusive that the audience is seldom conscious of the fact that a camera had anything to do with it." By contrast, Huston is confining and static, relying on pyramidal compositions and "close three-figured shots."

Huston's staging does leave his actors little room to move. One shot from *Key Largo* (1948) presents actors sliding into slots to create a "stiff" composition reminiscent of Welles (figs. 5.8 and 5.9). Yet what Farber dislikes in Huston's visuals is already latent in some of the pre-*Sierra Madre* films, such as *In This Our Life* (1942) and *Across the Pacific* (1942). At times *The Maltese Falcon* is as bold a depth-oriented film as *Citizen Kane*, and it dares some strange asymmetries that Welles doesn't attempt (fig. 5.10).

5.8 *Key Largo* (1948).

5.9 *Key Largo* (1948).

5.10 *The Maltese Falcon* (1941).

More generally, the rise of deep-focus cinema gave Huston plenty of competition for outré images. Many flamboyant shots were given us by cinematographer John Alton working with director Anthony Mann (fig. 5.11) and, quite a bit earlier, by production designer William Cameron Menzies. Oddly, Farber had praised Rudolph Maté's shooting in *The Pride of the Yankees* (1942). "With Maté, an expressive shot is never one that whams you over the head." But this comment ignores Menzies's eccentric shot designs (figs. 5.12 and 5.13). If any images seem either airless, clenched, or precious, it would be shots like these. Huston does have a fondness for aggressive compositions, but that's a more general tendency of the deep-focus aesthetic when applied to drama. On the whole, Farber considered Huston's crowded frames more unusual than they were.

Agee's 1950 *Life* profile of Huston came out after both of Farber's pieces. Rebutted in advance, Agee appears to have conceded some of his friend's points. Although he reiterates his praise (Huston's framing is "simple and spontaneous"), he does admit that the recent films show him to have become "more of a 'camera' man," with the result that the camera sometimes imposes on the story, the lighting becomes nearly arty, and "the screen at times becomes rigid, over-stylized."

5.11 *Raw Deal* (1948).

5.12 *Kings Row* (1941).

5.13 *The Pride of the Yankees* (1942).

Capriciously, Farber turned generous, calling *The Asphalt Jungle* "visually interesting and emotionally complex" and finding much to praise in *The Red Badge of Courage* (1951), which has its share of wide-angle depth. No matter. Huston's films had already provoked Farber to expose the depredations of the new Hollywood. His 1949 and 1950 pieces on one offending director launched his revaluation of the 1940s and put him on the scent of White Elephant Art.

For all his brawling energy, Farber didn't achieve Agee's level of renown at the time, but he did distinguish his critical voice enough to become a minority taste. Later he would be embraced by readers who savored his pungent defense of B films. His new fame was helped by his eagerness to write about contemporary European and avant-garde cinema for art mavens (in *Artforum*) and cinephiles (*Film Culture, Film Comment*).

What can we learn about 1940s film aesthetics from all this? The split decision on Huston opens up a problem in the Ferguson legacy. If two sensitive critics with so much in common can't agree on when a director is doing smooth, straight work and when he is showboating, how can we understand the distinctive features of American filmic storytelling? Was Hollywood cinema of the 1940s an era of expressive naturalism, integrating details with unassuming fluency, or was it an era of mannered filigree?

Both, I think. In every era Hollywood makes films in a plain style (whose norms shift somewhat) and others displaying self-congratulatory virtuosity (ditto). With Agee and Farber we have, for the first time, critics charting the arc swinging between forms of realism and forms of artifice. Just as important, Farber's exacting eye and bebop prose complemented Agee's moody lyricism in registering the power of Hollywood's exuberant creative ferment—a ferment that remained invisible to the *Partisan Review* critics of "mass culture."

On the other hand, who says we have to respect the Ferguson legacy anyhow? Maybe we should abandon honesty and naturalism and "continuity" and fluidity and all the rest? Parker Tyler gives that option a try.

6 *Parker Tyler*

A SUAVE AND WARY GUEST

Much that he says will disturb, horrify, enrage: there is no great audience yet prepared for an approach such as his, even to literature or to life, still less to the movies.

IRIS BARRY, PREFACE TO *The Hollywood Hallucination,* 1944

The opening of *The Young and Evil*, a 1933 novel by Charles Henri Ford and Parker Tyler, gives a fair sample of what is to come.

> Well said the wolf to Little Red Riding Hood no sooner was Karel seated in the Round Table than the impossible happened. There before him stood a fairy prince and one of those mythological creatures known as Lesbians. Won't you join our table? they said in sweet chorus.
>
> When he went over with them he saw the most delightful little tea-pot and a lot of smiling happy faces.
>
> A little girl with hair over one ear got up close and said I hope you won't be offended but why don't you dress in girls' clothes?
>
> The Lesbian said yes your face is so exquisite we thought you were a Lesbian in drag when we first saw you and for two long hours they insisted that he would do better for himself as a girl.
>
> He must have fallen asleep for he awoke with a start and saw a nice fat old bullfrog beckoning to him. . . .

The story's world is that of Greenwich Village bohemians and their gay/straight flirtations, affairs, and emotional double-crosses. The style is soft-core Djuna Barnes, with a hint of Gertrude Stein. Ford was only twenty, Tyler was twenty-nine, and they had already made names for themselves on the New York literary scene. *The Young and Evil* was refused by publishers in America and England and wound up being printed by the Obelisk Press, a Parisian firm known for erotica.

In 1934 Tyler published *Modern Things,* an anthology of verse by T. S. Eliot and other contemporary writers, including Ford and himself. One of Tyler's contributions, a free-verse piece called "Hollywood Dream Suite," ends with the image of box offices blown up. Tyler declared that his poetry aimed to transmit love through "a dream-convention" and "Rimbaudian hallucination." Early on, then, Tyler spun threads—homosexuality, gender masquerade, dreaming, hallucination, mythology—that would guide his journey through Hollywood movies.

Gore Vidal noticed. In his 1968 novel *Myra Breckinridge* a widow carries forward her husband's mission to write the definitive book on 1940s American cinema. Myra's guide is to be Parker Tyler's *Magic and Myth of the Movies* (1947). She writes in her diary, "Tyler's vision (films are the unconscious expression of age-old human myths) is perhaps the only important critical insight this century has produced."

Vidal's treatment of Tyler is partly respectful, partly mocking—in other words, fairly camp. *Myra* was a best seller (and in salaciousness went far beyond what Ford and Tyler had done), but its public surely had never before heard of Harrison Parker Tyler and his 1940s criticism. Vidal is said to have claimed: "I've done for him what Edward Albee did for Virginia Woolf."

If so, the effect didn't last. Tyler published essays and books on film, painting, and literature, and he continued to write poetry. My sense is that by the time of *Myra,* his fame, given a slight boost by the 1970 reprinting of *Magic and Myth* and *The Hollywood Hallucination* (originally 1944), was fading. Early on, he had associated himself with a gay/Surrealist avant-garde by cofounding with Ford the little magazine *View.* At the same period he endorsed experimental cinema, supporting the efforts of Maya Deren and life partnering with poet and filmmaker Charles Boultenhouse in 1945. He championed the European classics and the American mythopoetic cinema. But when the New York art world began celebrating the rise of Underground film, sanctified by the presence of superstar artist Andy Warhol, Tyler was dismissive at book length, calling the new films childish. Far ahead of his time in the 1940s, in the 1960s he was felt to be retrograde. He died in 1974.

Joining the Rhapsodes

Tyler is still an obscure figure compared with his contemporaries. James Agee and Manny Farber are celebrated as great critics, most visibly by volumes in the Library of America series, and Otis Ferguson occasionally attracts some minor tributes. I've been surprised how many people have told me they were unaware of Tyler's work.

That may be partly because he didn't straightforwardly accept the premises of what I've been sketching as the Ferguson tradition. Ferguson staked out a defense of Hollywood cinema based on its capacity for focused narrative presentation, driven by graceful movement, smooth continuity, and broad realism. James Agee and Manny Farber elaborated this premise by looking for moments invested with vivid emotion, poetic transcendence (Agee's specialty), and expressive details, either narrative or pictorial (Farber's).

Tyler tries something different. He's not a realist but a Surrealist. What Agee and Farber praised as "accuracy" or "authenticity" scarcely concerns him. And story—at least the story the film pretends to be telling—doesn't matter so much to him. The first chapter of his first book is titled "The Play Is Not the Thing."

Then there's his language. Reviewers of the time objected to it, which as one put it, "bears only a haunting resemblance to English." It's true that phrases like "Hepburnesque Garbotoon" are likely to disturb a *New Yorker* editor. But it's partly this hectic prose, far less conventional than his poetic diction, that gets him into my ecstatics club. He can riff with the best, although in just intonation and with minuet gravitas.

Veronica Lake, for instance, not only plays a ghost but looks like one.

> Although she is living, I have found something suggesting fright about her even in those roles in which she pretends to be a usual biological phenomenon. For instance, if there was ever a mannequin gangster, he was Alan Ladd in *The Glass Key*, and if he ever reached for the upper crust and took down a mannequin moll to load his mannequin gat for him, she was Veronica Lake. What in a less preternatural atmosphere might pass for restraint is in Miss Lake simple lack of animation; one is startled that she can talk.

Here is Tyler on Sinatra's appeal to the jitterbug.

> It somehow partakes of the schoolgirl's dream that a voice dripping with the most nectarish sauces should originate in a diaphragm over which the suitable screen would seem to be a large school initial surrounded by a sweater.

Or on Chaplin, in a book published the same year as Agee's homage to silent comedy:

> How well we know the image of Charlie in flight—turning a corner somewhat like a sailboat, frantically holding onto his hat and pivoting on the immobile axis of one foot, while the other leg, lifted high and bent, poises for the next stride, with the hand holding the cane at arm's length to maintain balance.

In a passage of simple eloquence that recalls Agee, Tyler meditates that even the fabricated piety of *Song of Bernadette* may legitimately evoke a world without killing and maiming.

> Peace, the normal pace of life, the relaxing rhythm of alternate rest and activity, the ritual embodied by all elaborately arranged movie scenes of sentiment, were these not supernatural indeed in a world paced by war and perpetual social crises? Sometimes the silence in the movie theater seemed fabulously exempt, and, as we snuggled into our seats, feeling that we in American cities were safe from bombs, the sense of some unnatural taboo might well have invaded us. Those actors on the screen, so careful and conscientious, privileged to choose an exact pace, allow an exact pause to dissolve, and never hurry . . . they seemed to have a supernatural leisure, to exist in the fabulous, sublime time of art.

All criticism is performative, but taken with my other Rhapsodes, Tyler makes forties movie talk a four-ring circus. It's time to reread him.

Mirror, Mirrors

Tyler wasn't in direct dialogue with Agee and Farber, but his work has a strong connection to one of the major ways of thinking about movies in his time (and ours). That is what we might call *reflectionism*—the idea that popular culture in some manner reflects the state of a society.

If movies are a mirror, what do they reflect? The simplest position is that they, like other mass media, reflect the tastes of their audience. Whether the filmmakers share those tastes or cynically play to them, Hollywood films' form and content answer customers' demands. Usually the audience's taste is held to be of surpassing vulgarity. In the 1940s this view was very common among intellectuals, shaped in particular by Clement Greenberg's essay "Avant-Garde and Kitsch."

A more sophisticated view is that movies reflect something broader— a current zeitgeist, the spirit of a time, the pervasive mood of the moment. Americans were feeling ultrapatriotic during World War II, the claim might run, so the moviemakers catered to them with movies that demonized the enemy and sanctified the American Way. Sometimes you get a different zeitgeist argument: movies that don't obviously reflect the temper of the times actually reflect it in their very refusal to talk about it. Hollywood offers "escapist" entertainment to make people forget their troubles. As presence or absence, the zeitgeist is embodied in the films.

Another version of reflectionism holds that films embody not passing moods but more enduring features of a society, something like national character. In the other arts, this is a long-standing explanation for certain traits, like the "heaviness" of German composers versus the "lightness" of French ones. Early historians of cinema saw German Expressionist films or Swedish landscape films as reflecting each country's temperament. From this angle, Hollywood movies can be said to "reflect" American optimism, practicality, and reverence for private property, along with more questionable values like the superiority of men to women and whites to other groups. This position was revived in more sophisticated form during the 1940s, when anthropologists like Ruth Benedict and sociologists like David Riesman tried to put the concept of national character on more secure foundations.

During the 1940s, yet another version of reflectionism became salient. Movies didn't merely embody mass tastes, or current concerns, or national character. What was being reflected was something partly hidden, even denied. (Probably an X-ray machine would have provided a better metaphor than a mirror.) A society's anxieties, concerns, and unresolved problems unwittingly find their way into popular entertainment.

The criticism associated with this view has come to be called symptomatic, because it treats films as involuntary expressions of things that society either ignores or suppresses. What the films reveal are not obvious endorsements of tastes and values but the traces of something more disturbing. The critic needs to decipher those traces.

For example, in 1946 Siegfried Kracauer suggested that *Shadow of a Doubt, The Stranger, Dark Corner*, and other thrillers betray a fear of the next-door neighbor and a fascination with psychological destruction. He inferred that "inner disintegration, whatever its stages, has actually become a widespread phenomenon." However chipper moviegoers might seem, deep inside they are fearful. Ultimately, Kracauer suggested, they fear the planned economy of the postwar years and associate it with Nazi totalitarianism.

Other instances of symptomatic reading draw more heavily on psychoanalysis. Sigmund Freud's influence had been growing in America since the 1910s and influenced literary interpretation, most famously in Ernest Jones's *Hamlet and Oedipus* (1910). Freudianism became particularly influential in the 1940s. It furnished both a popular explanation for how nations like Germany could "go mad" and a therapeutic technique that might help troubled people and traumatized veterans. It's not surprising, then, that books like Martha Wolfenstein and Nathan Leites's *The Movies: A Psychological Study* (1950) would hinge their case for recurring character types on the Oedipus complex and other syndromes.

By focusing on recurring character types and plot schemes, the symptomatic approach intersects with another trend of a reflectionist tint. Since the early part of the century, anthropologists who studied the myths of different cultures were finding common elements among them. Sir James George Frazer, in his monumental collection of studies *The Golden Bough* (1890–1915), traced a great many myths, including religious ones, back to fertility rituals. The idea was applied to literature by various scholars, most notably in Jessie Weston's *From Ritual to Romance* (1920). Frazer's cross-cultural search for recurring story patterns gained popularity later in such works as Lord Raglan's essay "The Hero" (1936) and Joseph Campbell's *Hero with a Thousand Faces* (1949).

Maud Bodkin's *Archetypal Patterns in Poetry* (1934) merged myth and psychoanalysis. She tried to explain the recurrence of myths by appeal to Carl Jung's model of mind. Bodkin saw plot, characterization, and even poetic imagery as presenting symbolic patterns that replay ancient stories and rituals, themselves embodiments of universal psychic processes. Jungians like Bodkin proposed that those patterns were inherited across generations and became embedded in our brains. In a more purely Freudian spirit, the critic and theorist Kenneth Burke believed that archetypes endured because as symbols they satisfied our unconscious appetites. Either way, one could imagine a synthesis of psychoanalysis and mythic interpretation.

As a fellow traveler of avant-garde New York painters and poets, Tyler was ready for this synthesis. Mythology and Freudian theory saturated French Surrealism, and American painters and poets followed the lead. *View* and its contemporary little mag *Chimera* owed a great deal to the

Surrealist émigrés who poured into New York during the 1930s. Abstract Expressionist painters copied the spontaneous approach to creation that Surrealists had tried with their "automatic writing."

Tyler thought that psychoanalysis and myth studies could illuminate popular culture, specifically movies. But he embraced no orthodoxy. He refused the patient explication of Jones and Bodkin and the theoretical flights of Burke. Nothing could be further from his project than the systematic method of Wolfenstein and Leites, who canvassed "all the American A-films with a contemporary urban setting which were released in New York City for the year following September 1, 1945."

Tyler makes no pretense of statistical precision or conceptual rigor. For instance, he appeals to a Freudian premise that I don't find in most of the reflectionists, the idea that a dream involves displacement of one image or element by another. But then he freely extends the idea of displacement to the audience, to shifts in camera position, and to other realms. Throughout his work, he stirred intellectually fashionable ideas into a powerful brew that risked tasting like moonshine.

He likewise had no ax to grind. Unlike Kracauer, Barbara Deming, and others, he didn't tsk-tsk. Tyler the critic liked movies, even when they were wildly distorting the world. Where others saw a grim mirror, he saw a sumptuous mirage.

Showing Off

For some it will be a tale of a boy and his dog. For others it will be much more. Rated G for those who think it's a tale of a boy and his dog, X for those who think it's much more.

1970S CINEPHILE JOKE

Tyler's work is distinctive for other reasons. He reviewed films occasionally, but only for little magazines and literary quarterlies, where his quasi-academic tone was welcome. He wrote on film at book length, something neither Agee nor Farber did. His books develop his ideas unhindered by word limits, and unlike the workaday reviewer he freely announces plot twists and gives away endings. Still, his two major books have a reviewer's air of contemporary coverage because he spins his ideas almost completely out of 1940s cinema.

The Hollywood Hallucination (1944) and *Magic and Myth of the Movies* (1947), however rambling they may seem, knot around several key ideas. Basic to Tyler's concerns, I think, is Hollywood's cultivation of collective moviemaking. High art in any medium, he says, requires that a single person's vision deliberately control the shape and implications of the work. A few films, mostly made outside America, meet this standard. Hollywood doesn't. American movies are group products, industrially manufactured and often casual and sloppy.

This view might seem to put Tyler firmly among the intellectuals who disdained mass culture. But he refuses to condemn American film.

> Hollywood is a vital, interesting phenomenon, at least as important to the spiritual climate as daily weather to the physical climate. . . . These judges [high-culture critics], unaware of the ritual importance of the screen, its baroque energy and protean symbolism, are unwarrantably summary, basically uneducated in the movie medium.

Hollywood films, aimed at the great public and allowing them a creative role as an audience, amount to something like a modern folk art, though one managed by greedy tycoons and adroit bureaucrats.

"Protean" is a key word in the passage. In the silent period, a D. W. Griffith or a Cecil B. DeMille could impose his vision on all of cinema's appeals, but by the time talkies came in, movies were closer to revue productions. Modern Hollywood, Tyler thinks, is show-offish. Anything— sets, costumes, performances, dialogue, fancy photography, even "realism"—is now a selling point. Dr. Tyler diagnoses Hollywood with an acute case of narcissism. It's endlessly fascinated by everything it does, and it invites us to enjoy its self-absorption.

Purity of form, in either classic or avant-garde art, must, he says, often slight qualities like "fullness or depth of feeling" and an adventurous use of the medium. These are things Hollywood is very good at achieving. Hollywood, banal though it usually is, gets so taken up with itself that it's always looking for something new to conquer, trying out gimmicks for their own sake. In the process, it arouses our emotions unexpectedly and reveals some important capacities of cinema as a whole.

Take the process of studio production. Contra the Culture Industry thesis, it's not perfectly regimented. At each stage, the writers, producers, director, actors, and editors are adding or subtracting elements, sometimes at whim. The result Tyler finds curiously "cubistic" and a very mixed bag. As the film goes along, details pop out at the expense of the whole, and a scene teems with digressions, loose ends, and momentary attractions. "Many a shot is a kind of three-ring circus, a contest for attention between the make-up man, the dialogue writer, and the star's personality."

Hollywood's narcissism shows up in another way. It's always replaying its own attitudes and activities in the movies themselves. Dorian Gray's fate in the film of Oscar Wilde's story is that of every movie leading man, declining from young god to sagging oldster. Or consider how the moguls treat the revered art of the stage. As everybody knows, Hollywood grinds up plays to suit its own formulas. Tyler takes as his example the movie adaptation of *Arsenic and Old Lace*. Here we are invited to enjoy the fun of unmanning the drama-critic protagonist. Bad enough, says Tyler, that he encounters his fear of impotence on his wedding night and so must constantly shoo off his bride. Worse, he's bound and gagged and must listen to a bad play recited by a would-be playwright, who happens to be a cop.

To top it off, in the original stage version the critic hates movies. So Hollywood punishes him by trapping him in his worst nightmare: what he'd regard as a bad film, the one we're watching, and liking. The movie capital exacts its revenge on New York snobs.

Did They or Didn't They?

Because of its urge to grab and flaunt whatever works, the Hollywood movie, Tyler claims, is a cinema of moments. Adorno thought that popular culture broke down traditional artistic form. Tyler grants the point but then scrutinizes the result: a texture pocked with gaps. The method of production creates "crevices for whatever there be in actor, dialogue, writer, cinematic trick shot, or directorial fantasy to creep through and flower."

A prime example of a crevice is the way films elide a basic fact: Did they have intercourse or not? He and she are alone together in a parlor or bedroom. If we're in the lush countryside, perhaps they're caught in the rain and take shelter. Fade or dissolve. Later, they're dressed as before, but *something has happened.*

A contemporary film would show us the Act. Thanks to strict censorship, American studio movies of the 1930s and 1940s can't do that. Yet entire plots can pivot around this Morality of the Single Instance. Can anyone believe that Irene Dunn, marooned for seven years on a desert island with Randolph Scott in *My Favorite Wife* (1940), didn't try out the horizontal mambo? Here and in many other films, the couple struggle to dissuade others from thinking they did it. But we can never be sure. You can call this Hollywood's absurd prudery, but Tyler enjoys it. By having it both ways the movie liberates our imaginations. It's as if there's one plot for one audience segment and a second, more obscure one for the spectator who wants more.

The star personas, the camera work, the music, the twists and inconsistencies of the story all activate "a perverse play of desires," but these aren't infinitely open-ended. Tyler believes there are limits on our recasting of the material we're given. Among those limits are the fantasies Hollywood has already woven for us. Our associational field is composed of the other movies we've seen, the fan magazines we've read, the larger funhouse of mass entertainment.

We submit to all this pinball-game impurity because it arouses some fundamental feelings. A film may lack the unity and power of a genuine work of art, but the illusionistic power of the medium and the hot materials churned together achieve a kind of "super-art." Anybody can see through Hollywood's tricks, but it's harder to recognize that they touch on essential concerns. "It is artifice. But beneath all these incredibly transparent artifices . . . is the ultimate fact of human lives, human desires, human movements, human etiquette." Sometimes sheer motion releases bursts of feeling, as in the sleigh ride in *A Woman's Face*, which kindles terror independent of the story situation. But other ultimate facts go deeper. The super-art of Hollywood movies has many "transparent artifices" that we spontaneously embrace.

Start with the actors, whom Tyler considers central to the Hollywood hallucination. (He almost never mentions directors.) Are the stars acting? Mostly not. They're playing a game of charades.

In charades you're assigned a word, name, catchphrase, or title. Without using sound you must pantomime clues that lead your team to guess the answer. For Tyler, this is what goes on in a film. We know the actor is really Gary Cooper or Joan Crawford, and we must intuit what's going on in heart and head based on the performer's approximate mimicry. A charade depends partly on fixed signs, like tugging your ear to indicate that this clue sounds like the secret word. Actors likewise emit stereotyped signs of emotion—the furrowed brow, the smile that fades.

In charades, when your friend mimics a ballerina or a tennis player, you never forget who he or she is. And the player's personality will inform the mimicry: a book lover will tend to associate famous novels with the clues. Similarly with movie stars. They pantomime the plot as required, but they often impose their own star personas on the role. Gary Cooper, playing Lou Gehrig as the script demands, sooner or later reduces the ballplayer to "Gary Cooper again." But this narrowing of dramatic possibilities (every film character becomes a variant of some star's persona) is compensated by "the fun, the plain lack of seriousness in the cinema charade."

There's more fun in store, because charades depends on associations. The weird, silly guesses your team members venture are essential to the pleasure. This is what happens when we watch a film, Tyler thinks. Like members of the charade performer's team, we engage in "a fluid guessing game." Hollywood filmmakers coax us to summon up a welter of more or less disconnected meanings and feelings. Once you notice these hovering implications, they can become as amusing as watching your teammate, assigned to pantomime *Bangkok*, stray into the naughty bits. In fact, straying into the naughty bits, such as the Morality of the Single Instance, is exactly what Tyler expects the wise critic to do.

The idea of the charade extends to voices as well. Close your eyes while watching a movie, and you'll conjure up "an independent medium of artistic illusion," he says. This is presumably one reason American movies became more of a mélange after the coming of sound. The voice not only enhances the star's "charade silhouette," it allows a new realm of accessory pleasures, perhaps veering off from the machinations of the plot.

Sometimes the voice overtakes the actor, as in the case of Frank Sinatra, who was known at the time as the Voice. "The Voice is the ventriloquist; Frank is the glamourized dummy." For Tyler, Lauren Bacall's smoky intonation (with its "special, fire-extinguisher kind of charm") becomes a blend of Marlene Dietrich, Greta Garbo, and Mae West, with a dash of jive singer Ella Mae Morse (of "Cow Cow Boogie" fame). "Here was Miss Morse's looping contralto lyricism lassoed into tacit, sophisticated prose."

Tracing out this penumbra of associations is part of the critic's role in the charade. So is noting that both Bacall's role and her debut performance in *To Have and Have Not* perfectly reenacted her audition for a studio part and prefigured her role as the new leading lady in Bogart's offscreen life. The Hollywood Hallucination constantly turns back on itself, so that our imaginations are encouraged to play among other manufactured images, both onscreen and off.

Sometimes Tyler is alert to the moment when the crevices open not into the world of movies but into our lives. He dares to ask of Frankenstein's monster: "Does he not ghoulishly reappear among us as the physically, mentally, or socially deformed ex-soldier?" This isn't authenticity of the sort prized by Ferguson, Agee, and Farber. It's more disturbing.

Tyler notes that many of the wartime combat films include actors who haven't yet fashioned a star image. (This reflects the fact that many of the biggest male stars signed up for military service and the studios thrust fresh faces before the cameras.) Tyler finds something moving in the way the camera records these beginners' fear of failure on three levels—as characters facing a mission, as actors trying to prove themselves, and as Uncle Sam's potential cannon fodder.

> Some of the most convincing acting in Hollywood has been by young men in the roles of military novices. . . . These young men, indulging in their waxen make-believe but virtually heroes as yet only in the Madame Tussaud sense, could measure in their imagination the spiritual cost of offering to sacrifice their lives if and/or when called upon for actual fighting. . . . Granted they were ambitious actors, they could intuit an odd parallel in the less familiar and less desirable training of a soldier preparing to go to the front.

Somnambules and Good Villains

The Hollywood charade offers a fairly small repertory of roles, and a good part of Tyler's first film book is devoted to tracing them out. The purest male hero, he suggests, is the unsullied young lover romancing his female equivalent. The hero has his faults, but they're forgivably human. Another heroic figure is the Benefactor of Mankind, the self-sacrificing inventor, scientist, or crusading doctor.

A more interesting protagonist is the Good Villain, "the sympathetic bad man." As either a gangster or a beloved rogue like Raffles or Don Juan, the Good Villain is a vigorous figure who attracts our admiration. He expresses his desires and emotions through direct action. He violates the law but he can't understand why he deserves punishment. To some extent neither can we. Tyler notes that the source of the hero's flaw is kept vague (bad luck, social conditions), the better to abandon us to our own imaginings.

Then there is the Bad Hero, the man with a significant character flaw. A mild example is the bashful bumpkin played by Gary Cooper and his peers. He's tainted by his backwoods ignorance, but he charms us because Hollywood, mysteriously, treats gullibility as supremely human. The more thoroughly Bad Hero is a rare figure in Hollywood because the need for a happy ending can't endow him with the stature of the flawed, fated protagonist of classic tragedy. An Oedipus is unwelcome.

Tyler finds that some films try to create a Bad Hero out of a Good Villain. Sam Spade in *The Maltese Falcon* is virtually "a stock villain held in the hero's place," not least because of Humphrey Bogart's earlier gangster roles. Yet as a detective who carefully steers between flouting the law and upholding it, Spade presents a "complex emotional struggle" akin to that found in Dostoevsky and Kafka, even if he turns naively sentimental at the end.

Somewhat similar, Tyler thinks, is another exemplary protagonist: Charles Foster Kane. Ferguson and Farber criticized *Citizen Kane* on grounds of muscle-bound technique and emotional coldness. Agee considered Welles more a skillful entertainer than a probing artist. Tyler's objections overlap a bit with these; he complains that Kane is pumped to colossal size chiefly by studio production values. More crucially, he notes that the film tries to give tragic depth to a stereotyped bad guy, the ruthless captain of industry. Kane is purportedly a man driven by lost love who finds only frustration and isolation. The film wants the impertinent Charlie of the early reels, a roguish Good Villain, to turn into the rigid Kane, a Bad Hero facing an end he was destined to create. For Tyler, though, "Rosebud" becomes a mechanical gimmick, and Kane's shallow mind is displayed in his indiscriminate art collecting and his promotion of his mistress as a diva. The characterization reveals Hollywood's melodramatic conception of overmastering passion. Teasingly, Tyler suggests that the film could have usefully borrowed the plot device of Chaplin's *Great Dictator* and split Kane into two: the dictatorial millionaire and the young actor trying to impersonate him, both played by Welles. "Then, at least, we would have had comedy."

Women have their charade roles too. The silent era was dominated by the Vamp and the Canary (the fluttery virgin), but sound cinema brought a new category, the somnambule or sleepwalker. This is the woman who floats through the film in suspended animation, dreamily prepared for sexual consummation. She may be an exotic import, like Garbo or Dietrich, or American cousins: the "neurotic somnambule" Bette Davis, the showgirl Hedy Lamarr, and the stripper—the "minimum role" for a somnambule. Mae West, Tyler ingeniously proposes, combines all these and adds a dash of female impersonator.

Wolfenstein and Leites's 1950 book proposes blander, sterner stereotypes of movie characters, such as the Good Bad Girl. These routine figures play out the Freudian skit of daddy, mommy, and me. Tyler's repertory of types seems to parody those roles in advance, while he looks for more cryptic clues and a murkier sexual pathology. The male roles are aggressively masculine, a response, Tyler says, to "female sexual excess." At the limit, Frankenstein's monster is a lumbering symbol of rape. Meanwhile, the somnambules are hypnotically prepared by men for sexual surrender. Even the willful Scarlett O'Hara is enraptured by the Technicolor presence of Ashley Wilkes's clothes, accent, and head.

Tyler's second book, *Magic and Myth of the Movies*, adds to the charade catalog by considering comedians and clowns. They openly exploit sexual uncertainties. Red Skelton, Bob Hope, and Danny Kaye play nervous males who are cowardly and effeminate; yet mysteriously they lust after women. The female clowns in their turn are brashly masculine, as seen in raucous Betty Hutton and homely Martha Raye.

In short, Tyler is no orthodox Freudian, stepping flat-footed through the Oedipus tango. He takes psychoanalytic ideas poetically, as a way to illuminate the subterranean currents gushing through a movie. He plays with weird possibilities as if constructing his own dream out of them. In *Of Mice and Men*, why not admit that George is Dr. Frankenstein, possessing a creature he controls sadistically, while Lennie is the monster who seeks not love but rape? Or that George is the dominant male, Lennie the pliant female in a vaguely homosexual couple?

In *Double Indemnity*, why does Neff record his confession for Keyes? Their friendship has an edge of male rivalry; the plug-ugly Keyes is clearly no gal magnet. As for Phyllis, who breaks up the couple . . . well, maybe she doesn't use sex to get the money but rather uses the money to get sex. And why does Mildred Pierce not understand what every audience member does—that her daughter is a spoiled bitch? Is it not best to think of the film as Mildred's wish-fulfillment dream, expunging a second husband and a wretched child from her life so she can return cleansed to her first husband, whose name she has never surrendered?

Psychiatry pervades 1940s film plots, as if Hollywood were eager to show that even apparently ordinary citizens can nurse murder in their hearts. So Tyler feels warranted in amping up the industry's narcissism. Unlike the mass culture scolds, he's not laying bare the dark soul of American culture. He's shocking and amusing himself, and us, with all the ways the critic can "reveal a weightier entertainment value in films than Hollywood itself is aware of."

Barbara Deming was annoyed at such frivolity. Couldn't Tyler see that his Hollywood heroes "lack a dynamic relation to society"? And that his single-instance lovers are cut off from a meaningful community? Deming wants to castigate Hollywood for its clichés, but Tyler finds in those clichés something sincere, poetic, and agreeably sinister. By treating interpretation as a game rather than a denunciation, he's able to suggest of *Arsenic and Old Lace*: "Itself a spoof of macabre monster movies, this film contains an inner dimension of zany fun within an outer dimension of zany fun."

Schlemiels, Schlimozzels, and Other Medicine Men

The Hollywood Hallucination treats the idea of film as dream both more and less seriously than the academics did. Tyler's follow-up book, *Magic and Myth of the Movies*, does the same thing with the idea of myth.

In his earliest writing on film he compares stars to the ancient gods and goddesses. This isn't just because they are worshipped by the multitude. The stars, he claims, fulfill long-lasting needs not met by contemporary religion. People like us, they are somehow immortal. On the screen they live and die and live again. Like the Homeric gods, they disguise themselves to us. They become cowboys or detectives, queens or saloon girls; but we recognize them every time. They reenact their roles so that each film becomes a ritual akin to ancient drama. Our gods, symbolically slain or beatified, populate stories that are magical invocations tailored to a modern Christian society.

Myth, Tyler explains, is "a basic, prototypic pattern" that reveals "imaginative truth." He's aware of Frazer's work, and he acknowledges that much of religion has a source in pagan tales and rituals. Like Maude Bodkin and Kenneth Burke, he finds that myth presents archetypes that speak to basic human desires. Speaking to those same desires is Hollywood's business, so the correspondence is enticing.

So far, so academic. But Tyler can't leave it at that. A secular society, he claims, fashions new myths. The movies give us, for example, the archetype of the absent-minded professor or inventor. The bumbling success of the awkward scientist, mocking efficiency but also proving that even fools can flourish in a democracy, is no less a myth, for Hollywood's purposes, than is Diana the virgin huntress (often incarnated, incidentally, in Katharine Hepburn).

Tyler's favorite myth in modern clothes is that of the medicine man. Far, far back, the king was the all-powerful figure. Eventually he split into the ruler and two other figures: the medicine man and the fool. Modern clowns share both functions. As fools, they make light of serious matters and seem "immune to normal human feelings." They behave obtusely, without alertness or social grace. But they also heal us by making serious things bearable. They are scapegoats who take on our vices so that we may laugh at them. And they have emotional depths. Charlie Chaplin's Tramp may wear a constant mask, but he is a real human who suffers like Pagliacci and then can start fresh, with a twitch of the mouth and a jaunty shrug and wriggle.

Tyler's breathless presentation plays loose with comparative mythology studies, but he defends his critique as no more of a farrago than the phenomenon he's studying: the results onscreen. In his "psychoanalytic-mythological approach," he explains, "I have only been obeying Hollywood's own law of fluidity, of open and ingenious invention." Once more American movies, as both less and more than a traditional art, demand a vision free from rigid doctrine, either Freudian or Frazerian. The films' dream logic reworks archetypes unpredictably.

Just as 1940s films turned toward presenting psychoanalysis, so did they dabble in magic. Angels, ghosts, witches, and other supernatural creatures flit through the lives of ordinary folks. Why? Partly because these creatures permitted filmmakers to revive the cinema trickery of films' earliest years, the hallucinations of Georges Méliès *et cie*, and marry them to current conventions of comedy and melodrama.

Thus *Turnabout*, derived from the coyly dirty mind of Thorne Smith (*Topper*), employs modern special effects to let a couple swap bodies in a gender masquerade with roots in superstition. The husband "mimics a certain type of homosexual," and the wife becomes "the horsiest variety of female." Alternatively, the already spectral Veronica Lake renders the father-daughter incest plot in *I Married a Witch* all the more piquant. When as ghosts she and her father are vacuumed into separate wine bottles, spirits infused into spirits, modern special effects revive the ancient motif of imprisoned genies.

These fairy tales are perverse but still comic. How does magic slip into more dramatic genres? Tyler's exhibit A is *The Picture of Dorian Gray*. It's based on the ancient superstition that a person's soul can be captured by an image. In this film Tyler finds a fascinating blend of all his favorite themes. We have Narcissus in Hurd Hatfield's beautifully vacant face, "a passive, dreaming mask." Hollywood practices its usual blunt-instrument surgery by turning Wilde's tale of love as an aesthetic pursuit into a romance between Dorian and "a doll-faced chit."

But the film compensates by creating "the first male erotic somnambule who is a beauty." Dorian becomes an image, drifting through his mansion as if a ghost himself. The painted portrait, sensationally tawdry, conjures up the iconography of Dracula and other creatures of the night, while Dorian's decay sums up the fate of every matinee idol. As ever, Hollywood recruits myths both old and new, magic and superstition from all eras, in order to present a cascade of arresting moments that tease us toward other images, other stories in its treasure house.

From all these sources Hollywood feeds its narcissistic energy. It can tailor myth and superstition to suit its stars and scenarios. But it will curtail the somber side of myth. Imbued with Christian values, in which the Son of God redeems suffering, Hollywood is committed to the happy ending. The drama's context is social, not cosmic; the conflicts involve not morality and unsettling self-knowledge, but merely law, custom, and proof. Is our hero guilty as charged? Will boy get girl? Who is the real killer? What does "Rosebud" mean? Social harmony outweighs tragic fate.

As a result, the Hollywood ending, fully foretold, doesn't accumulate much power. Once more, genuine art's stringent purity of form is replaced by the compulsion to show off. The movie story is just a jumping-off place anyway, so the wrap-up can be perfunctory. Films like *Suspicion* tease us because they force us to ask about the real action, the stuff underneath and between the scenes. (Didn't Lina deny Johnny her bed when she began to suspect him?) The movies can therefore get by with a phony resolution. "When reality and entertainment are thus held identical, all endings are purely conventional, formal, and often, like the charade, of an infantile logic."

The Man of the Self-Made Myth

For critics of the 1940s, Griffith and Chaplin towered over the American silent cinema. When Griffith died in 1948, he was a purely historical figure. But Chaplin was still a public presence. His first two sound films, *City Lights* (1931) and *Modern Times* (1936), had found wide success and, along with a 1942 sound edition of *The Gold Rush* (1925), still circulated in revival houses. *The Great Dictator* (1940) split Chaplin into three: the Hitlerian Hynkel, the Jewish barber who resembles him, and Chaplin himself, pleading with his audience for tolerance.

Monsieur Verdoux (1947) signaled that the world's most popular film character was forever gone. The silent era that American critics revered was definitively over. What, then, to make of a film that turned the Tramp into a cynical killer of lonely women? Farber praised *Verdoux* in passing, and Agee wrote three long and admiring reviews. The most extended tribute came from Tyler, who devoted an entire book to the actor and his persona. *Chaplin: Last of the Clowns* (1948) was at the time a paradoxical pendant to Chaplin's career.

The book offers a more lyrical, diffuse meditation than we get in *Hallucination* and *Magic and Myth*. Fragmentary and repetitious, it surrenders to rhetorical questions and the last refuge of the undeveloped idea, the three forlorn dots of ellipsis. I confess myself mystified and bored by several stretches of the book. Still, it is studded with bons mots, and it gives Tyler the chance to expatiate on Charlie the Tramp, Chaplin the comedian, and Charles Spencer Chaplin the man, and the myths they all forged together.

The idea of Chaplin as mythmaker was already in the air, since it was easy to take many of the films as chapters in a continuous saga. Soon after Tyler's book appeared, another poet, Robert Payne, would publish *The Great God Pan* (1952), treating Chaplin as a reincarnation of that pagan deity. Tyler, adhering to the idea that myths were both ancient and recent, gave Charlie a more complicated genealogy. He finds that the Tramp blends several varieties of clown.

He is another medicine man, transmuted into a fool who will serve as a scapegoat for all our ills. Like the hunchback or mute jester, he is physically flawed, small but with big feet. Charlie is also Pierrot, the white-faced clown seeking love but doomed to betrayal. He's Pagliacci too, the clown who suffers while making us laugh. But thanks to cinema Charlie has gone beyond his predecessors. The others perform in a sacred space, before the tribe or on a stage, but his shoes carry him into Life, our time and place as captured by the camera. Once there, he can disrupt situations we know—pedestrian traffic, a spa, a roller rink, a theater performance, or a movie set. To the last of the clowns, cinema offers the world as a stage.

Charlie's legend is paralleled by Chaplin's no less mythical life. A biographer tells us that early in life he fell in love with a girl named Hetty, who was carried away from him in a car. This is all Tyler needs to get started. Hetty becomes the first in a long chain of displacements, those beautiful young women who aroused Chaplin's desire in life and in his stories. Courtesans drive away in limousine comfort in *A Woman of Paris* and *Monsieur Verdoux*, but just as often women are destitute, crippled, or abused. In both life and art Chaplin suggests Don Quixote, who hopelessly idealizes Dulcinea, but his mesmeric control over his leading ladies adds another literary myth, that of Svengali and Trilby. He adapts his legend and his life to modern times with imagery of the city, of machinery, of industrial capitalism and Nazi dictatorship. Throughout it all,

Charlie's dream of perfect love failed in Chaplin's private life as well as in his art.

We've already ventured into psychoanalytic territory, but Tyler is fearless in finding poetically shaded Freudian scenarios as he pries out bits from Chaplin's life and welds them to the films. Young Charlie learned pantomime from his mother, who loved to mimic their neighbors. His father, a failed music hall performer, died a drunkard when the boy was five. "The father-rival had failed in his duty," but the son would succeed.

Succeed at what? Making a lot of money, attracting admirers worldwide, and conquering women. But it's all incomplete, Tyler thinks. Gradually Chaplin was forced to scrutinize the dream that Charlie pursued. The Tramp might find love at the fade-out, but the artist did not. So in *Verdoux* Charlie becomes the suave lady-killer, a new version of Pierre in *A Woman of Paris* and all those Lotharios who stole the girl from the Tramp. Now, instead of losing the woman, Charlie as Verdoux wins her, brutally. "*The man of the world enjoys the woman and passes on, leaving her ruined. The ideal becomes the cast-off plaything.*"

Alternatively, near the end of the book, Tyler considers reversing chronology and treating *Verdoux* as not the end but the *beginning* of the Tramp saga.

> Let us presume Verdoux concealed more than one possibility in his dudeish person; let us assume this possible ego was as desperate as Verdoux but that he did not have Verdoux's vulgar adventurism, that he rejected the idea of victimizing women; that he was constrained to leave home and family, say farewell to the actual dream cottage, and become—not a murderer—but the genesis of Charlie the Immaculate.
>
> I say: Charlie, perhaps, was not born full-blown; that he had a past like anyone else. . . . Verdoux is . . . how Charlie came to be.

The book ends here.

Kracauer was outraged, and in a review he called the author a self-indulgent narcissist and the book "disturbingly fictitious." Tyler might have agreed. The Surrealists spoke of "irrationally enlarging" the films they saw. Tyler rummages through his imagination to generate another Chaplin saga, one that satisfies the hunger the movies have aroused in him and that, not incidentally, lets him once more demonstrate criticism as a performance art.

Mamma's Precious Boy

The spectator must be a suave and wary guest, one educated in a profound, naïve-sophisticated conspiracy *to see as much as he can take away with him.*

PARKER TYLER, The Hollywood Hallucination, 1944

What, finally, do *we* do in the movie house? Ideally, we join the game, play into the charade. Professional critics are too jaded to take a hand. "We must be the ghosts amid the reality of artistic fantasy."

Once we play with suavity and wariness, we aren't wholly at the mercy of the mirage. As in the Chaplin book, Tyler offers himself as evidence. "Yes, I have made up a collective myth of my own, and I confess that in so doing I have plagiarized Hollywood exhaustively." Let's take him at his word and track one of his homemade fantasies.

Alongside his 1934 poem "Hollywood Dream Suite" in *Modern Things*, Tyler published "Address to My Mother." The brief lyric ends,

> you dying, that the earth say so, but
> I, always pausing,
> feeling the weak quiver
> my eyes straight at you
> know a, no monument, no
> sign, but closed eyes you
> having lost your flesh before: live;

This elegiac sentiment is echoed in *Magic and Myth*, which is dedicated to his father and "the memory of Eva Parker Tyler, my mother."

Mother, coincidentally named Eva, in some sense *equals* the movies, as we good mythomanes discover. Look at the hypothetical example of guilt that Tyler supplies in *Magic and Myth*: a little boy raiding the jam jar when mom comes in. Recall as well that Tyler saw the wellspring of Chaplin's pantomimic genius in his urge to imitate, and please, his mother.

Then we come upon the gentlest passage I know in Tyler's 1940s criticism. It celebrates the moment in *Gung Ho!* (1943) in which a select platoon of marines is berthed in a submarine headed to a deadly confrontation with the Japanese. The men sweat and quarrel in the claustrophobic heat. They strip to the waist and stretch out on their bunks. Trained to move, they must "sit tight—and simmer." The situation has, Tyler says, "peculiar and suggestive poetry."

6.1 *Gung Ho!* (1943).

For as we see the naked, perspiring flesh of these youths, softened by the coincidental presence of their identification tags necklacing their chests, their military mold is visibly relaxed, as though the heat of the closed submarine caused to melt the less resistant metal of war that has become part of their bodies even as it has forced them to remove the rigid encrustation of war, their unmelting military paraphernalia. The spirit of war seemed to have reduced them to one substance. . . .

Passive as babies, they begin to show their worry and fear (fig. 6.1). Each knows he may die in the battle to come.

They were returned to a state of childhood, and for these boys it was naturally to that state when, depending on their mother's benevolence, they were accustomed to ask bounty and loving protection from her. So their faces assumed that mask of innocent and pure appeal that little boys wear specifically to attract and compel the good will of their mothers. There is something infinitely calculating and hypocritical about this automatic mask. . . . But the

impulse to appeal to something is very strong; hence by the meta-
phoric bridge of the submarine as a womb they reach their mothers and through their mothers an image of overhanging nature, to
which, as the blue sky, warm sunshine, and invigorating air, from
which they are now farther away than ever, they make a humble
appeal, automatically dictated by the type of innocent guile they
practiced on the maternal being—their spontaneous charade of
being mamma's precious boy to whom nothing can be denied.

In this connection, I think, we must linger upon Tyler's account of Mae
West. He pays tribute to "the scandalous sway of Miss West's hips—it
reminds me of nothing so much as the motion of a cradle." Admittedly,
Mae is cruel to her little boy. In masquerading as a female impersonator,
she robs that figure of his comedy, "leaving him only his pathos." Still, in
that gesture Mae also enacts

the one supreme sacrifice of female nature: the mother's recognition and condonement of the homosexual flaw in her son! This, of
course, almost never happens in life; that is why it had to happen
at least once in art.

That passage occurs in *The Hollywood Hallucination*, which bears this
dedication: "To the memory of my mother, that golden nature whose
image so often illuminated with me this side of the movie screen."

7 *Afterlives*

A moment comes when everything is exactly right, and you have an occur-
rence—it may be something exquisite or something unnameably gross;
there is in it an ecstasy which sets it apart from everything else.

GILBERT SELDES, *The Seven Lively Arts*, 1924

I've confined this book to the forties, dipping back to the late 1930s to take Ferguson's full measure. It's now time, in short compass, to assess the later work and long-term legacies of my Rhapsodes.

I wish I knew more about how these four critics, all based in New York, got on with each other. They haunted overlapping spheres of bohemian arts and politics. Ferguson would have mocked Tyler's arty milieu, but it's not impossible that they attended the same MoMA or revival screenings. Farber and Agee were friends, but did they go to movies together? Both reviewed Maya Deren's 1946 screenings of her films in Greenwich Village. Very likely Tyler attended those as well, since he acted in *At Land* and *Ritual in Transfigured Time*.

Mostly we have to rely on the published record. Farber at this period never mentioned his counterparts, though in later decades he had things to say about Agee and Ferguson. Tyler, similarly, ignored the others until in 1971 he called Agee America's greatest film fan. In 1946 Farber wrote an insulting review of Deren's work, which may explain why Tyler ignored him ever after.

Agee was more generous. He mentioned Farber occasionally, and sometimes he carved out a Farberian sentence: "[*Stage Door Canteen*] is a nice harmless picture for the whole family; and it is a gold mine for those who are willing to go to it in the wrong spirit." (Paraprosdokian again.) Agee also refers directly to Tyler when speaking of Deren's film lyrics. In the year that Tyler postulated Hollywood's starlets as somnambules, Agee seems to have picked up the cue, speaking of his beloved Elizabeth Taylor as having "a natural-born sleepwalking sort of guile."

Following On

Agee's wide fame as a critic came posthumously, with the 1958 *Agee on Film* collection. As we've seen, it triggered other collections in the 1960s and 1970s, and the success of the genre benefited Tyler and Farber.

Both had continued writing, about film and other things. Tyler, always the practical belletrist, could turn out copy to order. He produced slim but informed monographs on French painters, as well as a biography of poet Florine Stettheimer (1963), a study of heroes in literature (*Every Artist His Own Scandal*, 1964), and a monumental, gossipy life of Pavel Tchelitchew (1969). His film interests didn't flag either. The picture book *Classics of the Foreign Film* (1962) was in tune with America's emerging interest in French, Italian, and Swedish imports, and it inspired many a cinephile baby boomer.

He was quick off the mark with his own essay collections. Only two years after Agee's anthology, Tyler put out *The Three Faces of the Film* (1960). He updated it in 1967 and followed with *Sex Psyche Etcetera in the Film* (1969). The long out-of-print *Hollywood Hallucination* and *Magic and Myth of the Movies* were reissued in 1970. In 1971 Tyler added to the British edition of *Magic and Myth* a chatty introduction that staked his claim as the originator of dream-oriented film interpretation.

While working on his art-making, Farber returned sporadically to reviewing. After his stint at the *Nation* and a short stay at *Time*, he wrote art criticism and reviewed films for various magazines, including the *New Leader* (1957–59), *Cavalier* (1966), and *Artforum* (1967–71). He published long-form essays in venues as varied as *Commentary*, *Commonweal*, and *Film Culture*. From his 1950–71 output he drew nearly everything he included in *Negative Space* (1971), the anthology that introduced him to the auteurist generation. "The Gimp," "Hard-Sell Cinema," and "White Elephant Art vs. Termite Art," along with essays on Hawks, Walsh, and Sturges, came to define the Farberian ethos and aesthetic.

Both critics closed their critical careers in the 1970s. After collaborating with Patricia Patterson on essays on avant-garde cinema and New German Cinema, Farber ceased writing in 1977 to devote himself wholly to teaching and painting. Some of his paintings are dotted with references to films and his film criticism. Tyler aroused the ire of the avant-garde with *Underground Film: A Critical History* (1969) and proposed a curious account of cinema's poetic powers in *The Shadow of an Airplane Climbs the Empire State Building: A World Theory of Film* (1972). Meanwhile, as sexual mores were changing, he wrote frankly and amusingly about varieties of eroticism in *Screening the Sexes: Homosexuality in the Movies* (1973) and followed it up with *A Pictorial History of Sex in Films* (1974). This last book displays some of the most lubricious photo pairings and captions you'll ever see.

The Pad as Playpen

The two men's late work intertwined in fascinating ways. Tyler's style became simpler but more loquacious, even pedantic. ("Perhaps in passing a definition of the aesthetic content of the term *tact* may be given.") Farber's writing became still more impacted and hermetic, jammed with adjectives and bursting with pinwheel associations that force you to either pause or skip on. Ozu's "rigidly formalized, quaint homeliness," he says, is "a blend of Calvin Coolidge, Blondie, and Mies's neo-plastic esthetic." I see the Mies and sort of see the Blondie (but is it the comic strip's mundane domestic crises, the wisdom of woman, the locked-down camera positions?). On the Coolidge reference I give up.

The most intriguing comparisons between Tyler and Farber, though, aren't stylistic. Each man devoted more attention to European cinema and the avant-garde, and in ways that echo their 1940s concerns.

The renaissance of the foreign film in the United States after World War II seized Tyler's attention, though in a typically contrarian way. In a 1950 essay he objected to the "cheap melodrama" of *Open City* and the "mere surface naturalism" of *Bicycle Thieves*. Instead, and long before it became a critics' darling, he picked *The Rules of the Game* as a brilliant work, at once social satire and tragicomic morality tale. He also found Cocteau's *Les parents terribles* an ingenious reworking of the Oedipus myth, one that exploited "a poetry of the deposed and vengeful matriarchic spirit."

In the years that followed, Tyler would construct a European tradition counter to Hollywood. That tradition is presented in its most schematic form in *Classics of the Foreign Film*. The table of contents seems to be cycling through the 1960 film-buff canon, from the MoMA classics (*Caligari, Last Laugh, Potemkin, Metropolis, La Passion de Jeanne d'Arc*) to the postwar imports (the neorealists, *Rashomon, Ugetsu, Hiroshima mon amour, Wild Strawberries, L'avventura, La dolce vita*). Actually, Tyler retrofits official classics to his interpretive tastes. In *Throne of Blood* he finds primitive magic; *Mädchen in Uniform* is "a chaste ode to sexuality." *Classics of the Foreign Film* revises his 1950 views of the neorealists, but on his own terms. What's valuable in *Bicycle Thieves* is not its realism but its function as "a lucid moral fable"; it even bears the ancient stamp of "an initiation rite." Even the most naturalistic work may harbor form, artifice, and poetic evocation, and it is these that make something a Tylerian classic.

In the early 1970s he revisited current European cinema, along with contemporary Hollywood, and found defiantly unchaste odes to sexuality. His books on sex and gender onscreen return to the polymorphically perverse themes that he dug out of 1940s Hollywood. He continued to read against the grain, so that *The Great Escape* and *Husbands* become "homosexual mystery stories" and *The Damned* becomes a gay charade. Yet now it seemed that filmmakers had read Tyler's first books; they were flaunting the scandalous desires that had been pleasantly sub rosa. With a jaundiced delight he surveyed the vicissitudes of the erotic instinct in *Senso, I Am Curious (Yellow), The Last House on the Left,* and scores of other films, high, low, and very low. The *Pictorial History of Sex in Films* suggests an aging connoisseur of erotica proudly flipping through his files and exhuming some prize images while offering outrageous commentary. "Taped down or strapped down, when your transsexualized doctor has dildo rape in mind, you're in for it." The book is, in short, a scream.

Many of the motifs he wrote about in Hollywood films became tropes of the American avant-garde. The somnambule, that vacant, succulent man or woman who drifted through Hollywood movies, reappears in so many 1940s films that P. Adams Sitney borrowed Tyler's formulation to describe an entire genre of "trance films." Similarly, it may be that Gregory Markopoulos's exploration of classical myth and Kenneth Anger's fascination with magic (that is, magick) owe something to Tyler's *Magic and Myth of the Movies.* Perhaps Tyler was more of a conduit for ideas circulating in artistic culture than a point of origin himself, but there remain some striking affinities between the 1940s and 1950s American avant-garde and Hollywood as Tyler described it.

Tyler worried that the carefully shaped psychodynamics and mythic dimensions of the classic avant-garde could be lost. The 1950 article defending *The Rules of the Game* praised the experimental films screened at Cinema 16, but he issued a warning. "The danger of the experimental cult is formlessness and lack of a wide artistic culture. It needs discipline and more intellectual power."

Tyler thought 1960s filmmakers ignored his warnings. *Underground Film: A Critical History* examines the emergence of Andy Warhol, Jack Smith, Ken Jacobs, Michael Snow, and others in relation to the "classic" avant-garde. Tyler's book is not a complete demolition—his list of the Underground canon includes 1960s classics, from *Harlot* to *Star-Spangled to Death*—but it does plead for artistic standards, sophistication, and "firmness of outline." Underground films, he argued, were too shapeless because they relied on prolonged, free-form improvisation, usually in some loft. Thus was born the "pad film," a playground for the infantile exhibitionism of early Warhol and the "boredom unlimited" of *Wavelength*.

All the narcissism, erotic symbolism, and camp lurking in the crevices of 1940s studio films scampered into view in Underground films. "The slant on which I had first concentrated was now taking hold with people who made films rather than with people who *looked* at them." Joe Dallesandro and Jack Smith, Taylor Mead and Paul America, Edie Sedgewick and other purported superstars were in their druggy haze mocking the gods and goddesses of the classic years. In this negation, Tyler believed, the filmmakers were abandoning their responsibility to the true avant-garde tradition and to history as a whole. By the time he died in 1974 at age seventy, he had shaped that history, but the Underground considered him hopelessly out of date.

Double-Spaced

Unlike Tyler, Manny Farber remained largely uncaptivated by the postwar foreign-language imports. He praised a portmanteau release of three Pagnol, Renoir, and Rossellini shorts (*Ways of Love*, 1950), but he had no sympathy for *Miracle in Milan* ("moronically oversimplified") or *Rashomon* ("slow, complacent, Louvre-conscious, waiting-for-prizes"). Tyler's favorites, *The Rules of the Game* and *Les parents terribles*, went unreviewed by Farber, along with releases by Fellini, Visconti, Mizoguchi, Clair, Carné, and many others diligently covered by his contemporaries. The reason is, as usual, taste.

> The worst Hollywood B has more cinematic adrenaline than most English or French movies, and no one is more eclectic than the English director Olivier, reactionary than the Frenchman Pagnol, victimized by easy sensibility than the Italians De Sica and Rossellini.

Farber's distaste continued into his early and mid-1960s pieces. Godard offered "complex boredom," Fellini treated bit players as "wasteful clutter," *Red Desert* was "a silly film." The 1967 New York Film Festival offered him a bleak buffet of new European entertainment characterized by "the character who is no deeper, no more developed, prepared, explained than the people in fashion advertisements."

But soon Farber discovered Warhol and Michael Snow. The pad films that Tyler found shallow and narcissistic seemed to Farber, in 1968, adventurous. Warhol, surprisingly, earned Farber's prize adjective: his close-ups were "virile." Thereafter Farber found *Wavelength* "a pure, tough forty-five minutes," while Joyce Wieland's films reminded him of Manet and Caravaggio.

Farber's interest in the avant-garde, coinciding with his new assignment as film critic for *Artforum* in 1967, seems to have led him to reappraise recent Europeans. Soon, with Patricia Patterson, he was writing career appreciations of Godard, Buñuel, and Fassbinder (whom he considered akin to Warhol). Later the two would champion Herzog, Duras, and Straub as well. Farber planned, but didn't complete, a book on the young German filmmakers.

What joined the worthwhile Europeans to the American experimentalists was a concern with fresh articulations of space. Farber's critical calling card became his claim that a self-conscious sense of space, in both literal and metaphorical senses, was a defining feature of contemporary cinema.

By the end of the 1940s, Farber asserted, Hollywood's concern for intricate visuals had begun to overtake narrative clarity and expressiveness. This was one thrust of his critique of Huston, Stevens, Kazan, and other Gimp / White Elephant stylists. Now an image with "more grip per square inch than ever before" was ruling both Hollywood and alternative cinemas. In *The Graduate*, *Persona*, *Red Desert*, and other films, "the design play becomes as important as the story theme. As seldom happened in pre-1960s naturalism, the movie is constantly drumming a pattern in which dominant and subordinate are contested."

Against this trend Farber sets filmmakers who define a particular space for each project. Chabrol finds a "measured flow" for *La femme infidèle*, while *Touch of Evil* presents an allegorical space of disorientation and grotesquerie. Fassbinder uses "flat, boldly simple formats. . . . Fassbinder's intense shadowless image is not like anyone else's." Most exemplary is Godard's career, "a movie-by-movie exploration of one image or another."

In a curious way, Farber's concern with framed space crops up at the same time that Tyler criticized the passive Underground camera for ignoring the way editing could create new forms of space (and time). But Farber suggests that a film's space includes more than the field of view on the screen. It encompasses the actor's performance ("psychological space") and "the area of experience and geography that the film covers." As for negative space, he redefines that 1940s concept as a sort of synthesis of what the filmmaker supplies and what the spectator adds. I take this as a metaphorical parallel to the solid masses and dynamic relationships that the term summoned up for Hans Hofmann and his acolytes.

Another twist: While Tyler was publishing a great deal on post-Impressionist painting, Farber gave up art criticism for art practice but continued to focus his unique art-historical sensibility on films. Scattered through the late essays are dozens of references to painters both classic and modern, something we almost never find in his early film writing. Hollywood's expressive naturalism had made it proudly distinct from other visual arts. Now, with filmmakers fretting over the look of each shot, Farber was constantly reminded of Rothko, Johns, Vermeer, and other masters of plastic values.

The new generation's sensitivity to space, free of the exaggerations of 1940s and 1950s white elephant directors, made them legitimate inheritors of pictorial traditions. Yet the art-historical debts of the moderns didn't cut them off from their cinematic heritage. The 1940s remained Farber's point of reference. *The Wild Bunch* yields "a virile ribbon image"; *Kaspar Hauser* reminds him of Sturges. One moment in *Taxi Driver* echoes *Odds Against Tomorrow*, and another scene turns Travis Bickle into Cary Grant. Like Farber's allusions to bygone comic strips, these comparisons create a ricochet dialogue between Old Hollywood and contemporary cinema.

Farber stayed in touch with the 1940s in another way. Before he ceased writing in 1977, he and Patterson signed tributes to Howard Hawks, Raoul Walsh, Don Siegel, and Sam Fuller that blended his gimp-and-termite arguments with the new sense of directors as impresarios of space. In a way, the essays show the writers joining the auteurist debates of the period. At the same time, these pieces tie the directors to artistic traditions outside movies. Walsh recalls Brueghel, Siegel evokes Robert Frank.

Reckoning

The classic avant-garde versus that of the Manhattan Underground; the postwar foreign imports versus the new Eurocinemas of the late 1960s: These realignments gave Tyler and Farber fresh prominence. By focusing on their beginnings I may have given short shrift to their later, greater fame. But there's also a value, I think, in seeing that their better-known "mature" positions have sources in the earlier years.

In those years, along with Ferguson and Agee, they forged an aesthetic approach to American film. The reach of their imaginations and the sheer dazzle of their prose made a case, against all the skeptics who disdained Hollywood as a factory of mass delusion, that something deeply artful was at the base of studio cinema.

They deplored much of what they saw as routine and shabby. But they also discovered fluent storytelling methods (Ferguson), poignant expression (Agee), unassuming pictorial intelligence (Farber), and cracks opening onto myth, black magic, and sexual fantasy (Tyler). They raised our awareness of conventions, not in a crudely demystifying way, but by treating them as enabling moments of depth, vigor, and impact. In a tradition that always swung between artifice and realism, Hollywood filmmakers found new methods of artifice and new approaches to realism, and our critics responded with skeptical sympathy.

Considering all four is important, I think, for a balanced picture of Hollywood then and now. Current nostalgia for the studio years tends to favor the hard, cynical pictures. The cult of noir and of murderous bad girls has little room for the gentleness of *Happy Land* or *The Yearling*. We need to be reminded of *Dumbo* and *Intruder in the Dust*. If today more people enjoy Hawks than Ford, or Raoul Walsh than Clarence Brown, or *His Girl Friday* than *The Shop around the Corner*, that's partly because our tastes favor swaggering aggression (look at our current pantheon, from Martin Scorsese to Paul Thomas Anderson) over modest virtue (*Wreck-It Ralph, The Secret Life of Bees, We Bought a Zoo*). It's not surprising that Farber is the most popular of the Rhapsodes today; his 1950s persona favored tough pictures. But in his early days he was very open to the poignancy and romantic passion of some films. Ferguson was never ashamed to call a movie sweet or lovely, Agee could defend *The Human Comedy*, and Tyler appreciated that *The Song of Bernadette* and *Gung Ho!* could move ordinary viewers. All four were better attuned to the tender side of studio pictures than most of us are today.

These writers activate so many aspects of the classics, and they draw our attention so vigorously to striking films now largely forgotten, that I'm surprised they didn't flag other things that pop out for us. They mostly missed the stylistic revolution of deep focus, the long take, and extensive camera movement. They missed what seem to us obsessive plot patterns—the man on the run, the woman entrapped, the doubts and guilts that assail the protagonists of war pictures, home front pictures, even neurotic comedies. They never detected that academic standby the crisis of masculinity, and they didn't notice the way postwar drama thrusts women back into the kitchen and the bedroom. Tyler is sublimely indifferent to directors altogether (except Welles and avant-gardists), while Agee and Farber largely neglect Preminger, Mann, Siodmak, Sirk, Fuller, and Ophüls.

Meanwhile, a more densely philosophical and analytical film criticism showed up in Paris. André Bazin and his cohort, kept from Hollywood releases during the Nazi occupation, were flooded by the pent-up stock of American movies. Primed by what they'd read, and gifted with exceptional intelligence, they noticed the new Hollywood stylistics of the long take, deep space, and narrative complexity.

There is nothing in American film criticism of the time to match the theoretical probing of narrational principles we find in Claude-Edmonde Magny's *Age of the American Novel: The Film Aesthetic of Fiction between the Two Wars* (1948) or the prescience of Pierre Bailly's meditation on the values of the lengthy, static shot in Welles and Hitchcock. French critics pointed out that what Yanks called crime melodramas could be considered in the Gallic tradition of film noir. While Tyler was psychoanalyzing Chaplin, and while Agee and Farber were quarreling about Huston, Bazin was writing analyses of Welles and Wyler that were unprecedented in their depth and precision. Christophe Gauthier notes that France's ciné-clubs held many prints, in both sixteen and thirty-five millimeter. As a result, Bazin, Rohmer, and their comrades could rewatch the films and study them to a degree that the Americans couldn't. A good portion of what we take for granted about Hollywood artistry of the 1940s stems from French cinephiles who considered scrutinizing films to be as natural as explicating literary texts.

Perhaps my Americans would, under more favorable conditions, have done the same. In their work we can glimpse ambitions to probe further. Farber gave lightning-sketch applications of art-school formalism. Ferguson's shot-by-shot analysis of *The Little Foxes* and Agee's interpretation of *Monsieur Verdoux* shadowed the New Criticism's urge to scrutinize the texture of a poem. Tyler's ransacking of myth and psychoanalysis looked forward to the "extrinsic" interpretations of art and literature that began to rule the academy in the 1950s.

But they never became abstract theorists, partly, I think, because sooner or later each one found himself comfortable with the sheer stuff of cinema. Tyler acted in films and lived for decades with filmmaker Charles Boultenhouse. Ferguson, the man who sat under Jess Stacy's piano, sharpened his appetite to learn movie craft by visiting a set. Agee went from writing imaginary screenplays to writing real ones, the latter as giddy with detail as the former. When Farber began teaching at the University of California at San Diego, he tickled the analytical projector like a needle-dropping DJ. The good critic, they seemed to assume, needs to know the medium as intimately as possible.

Every chapter of this book has risked attributing too much to critics. If there hadn't been films that tested the boundaries of cinematic storytelling, even the cleverest reviewers couldn't have written so zestfully. Without Darryl Zanuck and Dore Schary and Hal Wallis; without galvanizing performers from Humphrey Bogart and Barbara Stanwyck to Clifton Webb and Eve Arden; without superb writers from Dudley Nichols to Vera Caspary; without Capra and Stevens, Sturges and Welles, Huston and Wyler, Hitchcock and Wilder, Wellman and Walsh, Lang and Preminger, Mankiewicz and Lewton; without perversities like *The Picture of Dorian Gray* and *Salome Where She Danced* and *Turnabout*; without ambitious pictures like *Citizen Kane* and *The Story of G.I. Joe* alongside scores of superb A releases, sturdy programmers, and B films of implausible ambitions—without all this, the Rhapsodes would have had little to work with. The overpowering, exuberant, piercing, and nonchalantly crazy films of the 1930s and 1940s surely pushed them to go all out.

We discovered these writers late, after we had learned that film journalists could be intellectuals. I've hoped to show that they left us a fine legacy. Driven by deadlines and last-minute revisions, limited in ways we in the age of Google can hardly imagine, four extraordinary critics dared to think subtly and write with brazen verve about the phenomenon called Hollywood.

Acknowledgments

This book began as a lecture for "Narrative Theory and 1940s Hollywood," a seminar I taught with Jeff Smith in fall 2013 at the University of Wisconsin–Madison. Thanks to Jeff and all the members of the seminar for an enjoyable semester.

The essays originally appeared as entries on Kristin Thompson's and my blog Observations on Film Art (www.davidbordwell.net/blog). The series was immensely aided by information and images from Kent Jones, who is an outstanding critic in his own right. Many thanks as well to Patricia Patterson, who provided images for the web entries on Manny Farber.

As readers of this manuscript, James Naremore and Charles Maland were everything one could ask for. Both superb scholars, they gave me detailed advice that greatly improved the book. At the University of Chicago Press, Rodney Powell dealt with the project with great dispatch, partly owing to his unremitting love of classic film. Thanks as well to Alice Bennett, whose skillful copyediting helped me understand what I was trying to say.

Here in Madison, I benefited greatly from discussions with my longtime friends Jeff Smith, Lea Jacobs, Ben Brewster, and J. J. Murphy. I'm also grateful to Eric Dienstfrey for his help in rounding up sources. Kristin Thompson was there every time I needed encouragement and love.

Sources

Citing every sentence or phrase I invoke would necessitate a flurry of endnotes, so I've decided to provide more general bibliographical commentary.

The core sources for the four critics are collections of their works. Unless otherwise indicated, my citations come from these sources. Usually, when I cite an author on a particular film, you can use the index of the pertinent volume to find the reference. When it becomes useful to identify a particular piece otherwise, I'll refer to it below using the following abbreviations:

The Film Criticism of Otis Ferguson, ed. Robert Wilson (Temple University Press, 1971), referenced as *OF*; and *In the Spirit of Jazz: The Otis Ferguson Reader*, ed. Dorothy Chamberlain and Robert Wilson (Da Capo, 1997; orig. 1982), referenced as *OFR*.

James Agee: Film Writing and Selected Journalism, ed. Michael Sragow (Library of America, 2005), referenced as *JA*. *JA* reprints only a sampling of Agee's *Time* reviews, and some pieces included are not by Agee. For a complete collection of Agee's *Time* contributions see *The Works of James Agee*, ed. Michael A. Lofaro and Hugh Davis, vol. 5, *The Complete Movie Reviews, Commentary, and Criticism*, ed. Charles J. Maland (University of Tennessee Press, forthcoming). I'm grateful to Chuck for keeping me abreast of his work on that edition and for allowing me access to unpublished material.

Farber on Film: The Complete Film Writings of Manny Farber, ed. Robert Polito (Library of America, 2009), referenced as *MF*.

Parker Tyler's *The Hollywood Hallucination* (Simon and Schuster, 1970; orig. 1944), referenced as *HH*; *Magic and Myth of the Movies* (Simon and Schuster, 1970; orig. 1947), referenced as *MM*; and *Chaplin: Last of the Clowns*, referenced as *CC*. Since *HH* and *CC* are not indexed, I provide references to film titles mentioned in my chapters.

Many of the articles I cite are available online through various search engines and library collections, and many more can be accessed through

Unz.org, Google Books, and the websites of the *Nation*, the *New Republic*, and other periodicals. For portraits of the critics discussed in this book, go to www.davidbordwell.net/blog/2015/10/03/the-rhapsodes-return/.

Introduction

Auden's appreciation of Agee is in *The Complete Works of W. H. Auden: Prose*, vol. 2, *1939–1948*, ed. Edward Mendelson (Princeton University Press, 2010), 239. *Agee on Film* was reviewed by Richard Griffith, "Reflections and Images," *New York Times*, 16 November 1958, BR5, and by Arthur Knight, "Tales of Two Critics," *Saturday Review of Literature*, 20 December 1958, 9. The *Times* review compares Agee to Gilbert Seldes, who was one of the first writers to treat American cinema as a dynamic popular art. Seldes's major books are *The Seven Lively Arts* (Harper, 1924), *An Hour with the Movies and the Talkies* (Lippincott, 1929), and *The Movies Come from America* (Scribner's, 1937).

Quotations from Ferguson: movies smooth and fast-moving (*OF*, 39); bits flickering past (*OF*, 16). Harold Rosenberg's complaint about kitsch comes in "Pop Culture: Kitsch Criticism," in *The Tradition of the New* (Da Capo, 1994), 265.

For a wide-ranging survey of the US scene, see *American Movie Critics: An Anthology from the Silents Until Now* (Library of America, 2006), ed. Phillip Lopate. There was a more academic film culture in the 1920s and 1930s too. See Peter Decherney, *Hollywood and the Culture Elite: How the Movies Became American* (Columbia University Press, 2006), and Dana Polan, *Scenes of Instruction: The Beginnings of U.S. Study of Film* (University of California Press, 2007).

Agee had apparently considered collecting his film reviews at the end of the 1940s. He may have been encouraged by the anthologies from English critics that had come out after the war. One example was C. A. Lejeune's *Chestnuts in Her Lap, 1936–1946* (Phoenix House, 1947). Another was the work of James Agate, a bluff theater reviewer and memoirist who took pride in knowing nothing about cinema, an admission as charming as it was accurate. The reviews collected in two volumes of *Around Cinemas* (Home and Van Thal, 1946, 1948) exemplify Nabokov's observation, "Nothing is more exhilarating than philistine vulgarity."

There were more specialized and serious film writers at the period in Britain, notably at *Sequence* (1946–52), but that journal deserves discussion on its own. Somewhat parallel was French criticism of the period, which is surveyed in Antoine de Baecque's *La cinéphilie: Invention d'un regard, histoire d'une culture, 1944–1968* (Fayard, 2003).

1. The Rhapsodes

Ferguson on unsnobbish criticism (*OF*, 412); Tyler on the voice (*MM*, 248). See also Tyler, "Three Movies," *View* 1, no. 1 (September 1940): 3. Tyler's remark on Camp reading comes from the preface to the first British edition, *Magic and Myth of the Movies* (Secker and Warburg, 1971), 11. Barbara Deming writes of "scuffed-in" meanings in "The Library of Congress Film Project: Exposition of a Method," *Library of Congress Quarterly Journal of Current Acquisitions* 2, no. 1 (1944): 10.

An indispensable book on Farber, Tyler, and their cultural milieu is Greg Taylor's *Artists in the Audience: Cults, Camp, and American Film Criticism* (Princeton University Press, 1999).

2. A Newer Criticism

Agee's remark about being sort of a Communist is made in *Let Us Now Praise Famous Men* (Ballantine Books, 1960), 225. He touches on mass culture categories in "Pseudo-Folk," *Partisan Review* 11, no. 2 (Spring 1944): 219–22, reprinted in *The Works of James Agee*, ed. Michael A. Lofaro and Hugh Davis, vol. 2, *Complete Journalism: Articles, Book Reviews, and Manuscripts*, ed. Paul Ashdown (University of Tennessee Press, 2013), 357–63. Agee's critique of social science reflectionism is in *JA*, 277. My quotation from Tyler about democracy and *Meet John Doe* is in *HH*, 185. Ferguson's hokum remark is in *OF*, 7. Alfred Kazin's report on Ferguson's mockery of political idealists comes from *Starting Out in the Thirties* (Little, Brown, 1965), 31.

My quotation from Virgil Thomson comes from *Music Reviewed, 1940–1954* (Vintage, 1967), 75. The Cocteau dig is in *Mary McCarthy's Theatre Chronicles, 1937–1962* (Authors Guild / iUniverse, n.d.; orig. 1956), 109; the remark about *The Skin of Our Teeth* is on p. 54. My *Cat People* quotation is in Joy Davidson, "Screen Spookery," *New Masses*, 22 December 1942, 31.

A good introduction to the "cultural left" of the 1930s and 1940s is James Burkhart Gilbert, *Writers and Partisans: A History of Literary Modernism in America* (Columbia University Press, 1993). My Edmund Wilson epigraph comes from p. 88. In *Left Intellectuals and Popular Culture in Twentieth-Century America* (University of North Carolina Press, 1996),

Paul R. Gorman traces trends of 1930s and 1940s cultural critique back to earlier decades. See also Richard Pells's two strong surveys, *Radical Visions and American Dreams: Culture and Social Thought in the Depression Years* (Wesleyan University Press, 1984) and *The Liberal Mind in a Conservative Age: American Intellectuals in the 1940s and 1950s* (Harper and Row, 1985).

Macdonald's 1938–39 attack on Stalinist cinema is reprinted, with strategic alterations, in *Dwight Macdonald on Movies* (Prentice-Hall, 1969), 191–249. A late example of the anti-Communist *Partisan Review* intellectual who occasionally wrote about film is Robert Warshow. His essays are collected in *The Immediate Experience: Movies, Comics, Theatre, and Other Aspects of Popular Culture* (Harvard University Press, 2002; orig. 1962). Some would rank him with my four critics, but for my money he doesn't come close.

By 1950 there were about thirty-five American magazines and reviews publishing literary criticism and cultural commentary. See Morton Dauwen Zabel in *Literary Opinion in America*, 2nd ed. (Harper, 1951), 812–21. Many of these journals were affiliated with universities. I've emphasized the New York intellectuals around *Partisan Review*, which like the academic reviews hosted more belletristic essays than were found in weeklies like the *New Republic*. A survey of trends in the literary quarterlies of the 1930s and 1940s is Wallace Martin, "Criticism and the Academy," in *The Cambridge History of Literary Criticism*, vol. 7, *Modernism and the New Criticism*, ed. A. Walton Litz, Louis Menand, and Lawrence Rainey (Cambridge University Press, 2000), 269–321.

John Berryman remarks on "the desertion of Marxism" in "The State of American Writing, 1948: Seven Questions," *Partisan Review* 15, no. 7 (July 1948): 857. The same symposium is the source of the survey question about the threat of middlebrow culture, p. 855. Abundant reflections on the turn away from Communism and toward cultural critique can be found in a later symposium, "Our Country and Our Culture," *Partisan Review* 19, no. 3 (May-June 1952): 282–326; 19, no. 4 (July-August 1952): 420–50; 19, no. 5 (September-October 1952): 562–97. My Philip Rahv epigraph comes from the first installment, p. 310, and the quotation from David Riesman is from pp. 311–12. For more on Riesman's position, see *The Lonely Crowd: A Study of the Changing American Character* (Yale University Press, 1950), especially 311–67.

Clement Greenberg's "Avant-Garde and Kitsch" is available in Greenberg, *Collected Essays and Criticism*, vol. 1, *Perceptions and Judgments, 1939–1944*, ed. John O'Brian (University of Chicago Press, 1986), 5–22. Dwight Macdonald's essay on mass culture was revised and expanded twice, but the version I refer to is the original, "A Theory of 'Popular Culture,'" *Politics* 1, no. 1 (February 1944): 20–23. My McLuhan quotation comes from "Inside Blake and Hollywood," *Sewanee Review* 55, no. 4 (October-December 1947): 715. In his remarkable summing-up of the era, "The New York Intellectuals: A Chronicle and a Critique," in *Commentary* 46, no. 4 (October 1968): 29–52, Irving Howe argues that the attack on mass culture collapsed because its sweeping denunciations could not be developed; the portrait of an all-dominating popular culture offered "neither relief nor escape."

Virginia Woolf helped popularize the term "middlebrow" in her unsent letter to the *New Statesman*, published posthumously in 1942 in *The Death of the Moth and Other Essays* (Hogarth Press, 1942), 113–19. A widely read satiric account of the Brows is Russell Lynes, "Highbrow, Lowbrow, Middlebrow," *Harper's Magazine* 198, no. 2 (February 1949): 19–28. Lynes offered a follow-up in "Highbrow, Lowbrow, Middlebrow Reconsidered," *Harper's Monthly* 216, no. 8 (August 1967): 16–20. *Mass Culture: The Popular Arts in America*, ed. Bernard Rosenberg and David Manning White (Free Press, 1957), remains a useful collection of 1940s pieces. Interestingly, a 1945 article by Theodore Strauss declared both Agee and Farber highbrow critics writing "over-complicated" prose. See "No Jacks, No Giant-Killers," *Screen Writer* 1, no. 1 (June 1945): 7.

The quotations and summaries pertaining to Adorno come from Adorno and Horkheimer, *Dialectic of Enlightenment*, ed. Gunzelin Schmid Noerr and trans. Edmund Jephcott (Stanford University Press, 2002), 102, 103; Adorno, "On Popular Music," *Zeitschrift für Sozialforschung* 9 (1941): 17–48; and Adorno, "The Position of the Narrator in the Contemporary Novel," in *Notes to Literature*, vol. 1, ed. Rolf Tiedemann, trans. Sherry Weber Nicholsen (Columbia University Press, 1991), 31. See also Horkheimer, "Art and Mass Culture," *Zeitschrift für Sozialforschung* 9 (1941): 290–304; Adorno, *Philosophy of New Music*, ed. and trans. Robert Hullot-Kentor (University of Minnesota Press, 2006); and Adorno and Hanns Eisler, *Composing for the Films* (Oxford University Press, 1947). Ferguson's appreciation of Bix Beiderbecke is in *OFR*, 20.

For one example of the painter acting as "producer" heading a studio of craftsmen, see Peter van den Brink, ed., *Brueghel Enterprises* (Ludion, 2001). Glancing through the ten variants of Brueghel the Elder's *Netherlandish Proverbs* that were churned out by his son's studio (59–79), the reader might ask how to distinguish this process from the "pseudo-differentiation" Adorno and Horkheimer attribute to the modern culture industry. Remarkably, it seems likely that Brueghel the son never saw the father's original work but rather worked from a sketch the father left behind—a treatment or shooting script, we might say.

Many left intellectuals castigated Hollywood at the period. See Paul Goodman's film essays collected in *Format and Anxiety: Paul Goodman Critiques the Media*, ed. Taylor Stoehr (Autonomia, 1996), and James T. Farrell's celebrated denunciation, "The Language of Hollywood," *Saturday Review of Literature*, 5 August 1944, 29–32. For an alternative view, see Arnold Hauser, "Can Movies Be 'Profound'?" *Partisan Review* 15, no. 1 (January 1948): 69–73. Hauser says yes.

Randall Jarrell's objections to the technical bent of New Criticism are formulated in his 1952 essay, "The Age of Criticism," in *Poetry and the Age* (Vintage, 1953), 63–86. For an influential example of the sort of analysis that arose from new compositional procedures in music, see René Liebowitz, *Schoenberg and His School*, trans. Dika Newlin (Philosophical Library, 1949). Analyses of film scores include Lawrence Morton, "The Music of 'Objective Burma,'" *Hollywood Quarterly* 1, no. 4 (July 1946): 378–95; Frederick Sternfeld's "The Strange Music of Martha Ivers," *Hollywood Quarterly* 2, no. 3 (April 1947): 242–51, and "Music and the Feature Films," *Musical Quarterly* 33, no. 4 (October 1947): 517–32, on *The Best Years of Our Lives*.

The American critics of mass culture usually held an austere conception of modernism. Léger, Cocteau, H.D., Satie, Apollinaire, and other avant-gardists had seen virtues in the young medium of cinema, while Les Six and the Surrealists embraced Hollywood movies. Such artists, part of the less solemn side of modernism, found inspiration in popular entertainments generally. Even Proust wished he were well enough to visit the cinemas, and Joyce had considered a career running a movie theater.

Erwin Panofsky's defense of popular cinema as a folk art appears in "Style and Medium in the Motion Picture," in Panofsky, *Three Essays on Style*, ed. Irving Lavin (MIT Press, 1995), 91–125. This is the 1947 version of the essay, but slightly different versions appeared in 1936, 1937, and 1940, so it was a constant, if muted presence during the mass culture debates of the era. Mortimer Adler's Aristotelian analysis of Hollywood cinema was carried out in *Art and Prudence: A Study in Practical Philosophy* (University of Chicago Press, 1937); my quotation comes from p. 579.

Noël Carroll's *Philosophy of Mass Art* (Oxford University Press, 1998) reviews many of the issues here. For an account of the theory of sound cinema developed by Bazin and his peers, see chapter 3 of my *On the History of Film Style* (Harvard University Press, 1997).

3. Otis Ferguson: The Way of the Camera

Many of the chapter's references are to films and names that can be found in the *OF* index, but some *New Republic* pieces are not reprinted there. The *Riptide* review is "The Desert, the Dare Boys and Coney," 18 April 1934, 271; the *Yellow Jack* review is "Jack and a Giant-Killer," 8 June 1938, 131; the review of *Espionage Agent* is "Three for the Show," 18 October 1939, 301; the Maurice Evans zinger comes in "A Play, a Picture," 12 April 1939, 279; and the flirtation with Ginger Rogers is from "Men and Women," 22 June 1938, 188, the same page that contains the needling of Katharine Hepburn. Other tags and references: "smoothing everything out" (*OF*, 365); the cumulative power of a story (*OF*, 397); Hollywood's new language (*OF*, 39); Errol Flynn's stolidity (*OF*, 413); Cagney and O'Brien (*OF*, 6); editing in a dialogue scene for shifting emphasis (*OF*, 370); wipe-dissolves and Clark Gable (*OF*, 24).

On incompetent critics, see *OFR*, 48; on the critic's two tasks, *OFR*, 49. Ferguson's travel notes to Los Angeles are reprinted in *OF*, 417–58. The "sinking rats" line comes from *OF*, 215. Harold Ross's opinion of film critics is quoted in Richard Meryman, *Mank: The Wit, World, and Life of Herman Mankiewicz* (Morrow, 1978), 123.

I've drawn my information about Ferguson's life from Malcolm Cowley's memoir, "For Otis," *New Republic*, 1 November 1943, 625–26; Alfred Kazin, *Starting Out in the Thirties* (Little, Brown, 1965), 29–35; and the foreword to *OFR*, ix–xix. The tributes from young people to Ferguson are in the *New Republic* correspondence columns for 22 November 1943, 719–29, and 20 December 1943, 887. Jess Stacy's remark is quoted by Whitney Balliett, "Jazz: Otis Ferguson," *New Yorker*, 10 January 1983, 84.

Ferguson's jazz writings, published and unpublished, are extensively represented in *OFR*. His remarks on Teagarden and Teddy Hill are to be found there. His most complete account of changes within the jazz tradition is "Jazz in New York" (1939), *OFR*, 32–47. His thoughts on musicians' profiting from the war appeared in "Moneychangers in the Tempo," *New Republic*, 19 January 1942, 85, and his suggested discography was published as "Records: A Start on Jazz," *New Republic*, 9 February 1942, 205–7; the reference to Armstrong's records is on p. 206. The passage on swing comes from "Breakfast Dance in Harlem," *OFR*, 59. For a useful history of music trends in Ferguson's time, see James Lincoln Collier, *The Making of Jazz: A Comprehensive History* (Delta, 1978), 123–92.

On Stark Young's career see John Pilkington, *Stark Young* (Twayne, 1985). Young's review of *The Cradle Will Rock* appeared in *New Republic*,

19 January 1938, 310–11; my quotation about *Time and the Conways* is taken from the same piece. Young discussed cinema's shortcomings in "Madame's A," *New Republic*, 14 September 1932, 124–26. He expanded these views in response to a letter from Nancy Naumburg in "Screen Version," *New Republic*, 19 October 1932, 259–61.

André Bazin's claim that 1939 was a watershed year for classical cinema is made in "The Evolution of the Language of Cinema," in *What Is Cinema?* vol. 1, ed. and trans. Hugh Gray (University of California Press, 1967), 30–31. On Hollywood's continuity aesthetic, see David Bordwell, Janet Staiger, and Kristin Thompson, *The Classical Hollywood Cinema: Film Style and Mode of Production to 1960* (Columbia University Press, 1985), chaps. 5 and 15–18.

Peter Ellis's review of *The Baltic Deputy* appeared in *New Masses*, 14 September 1937, 28–29; Ferguson's is on pp. 196–97 of *OF*. William Troy's review of *M* appeared in *Nation*, 19 April 1933, 454–55; his review of *The Power and the Glory* is "Concerning 'Narratage,'" *Nation*, 13 September 1933, 308. See also his discussion of "Camera Wit," *Nation*, 17 May 1933, 567. Troy soon became a proponent of myth criticism, a trend taken up by Parker Tyler. Troy's original statement came in "Thomas Mann: Myth and Reason," *Partisan Review* 5, no. 1 (June 1938): 24–32, and 5, no. 2 (July 1938): 51–61. He defended his approach more abstractly in "A Note on Myth," *Partisan Review* 6, no. 1 (Fall 1938): 95–100. The best-known version of that piece, revised some years later, appeared in *William Troy: Selected Essays*, ed. Stanley Edgar Hyman (Rutgers University Press, 1967), 35–39.

Agee's remark about not wanting to know how films are made appears in his first *Nation* review (*JA*, 35). Fortunately for us, he changed his mind.

On *Penny Serenade* and figure 3.1, Ferguson didn't go on to mention that the opaque framing in this scene does other things. It harks back to the first scene's glimpse of a doll on the child's bed, it prepares us for a moment of suspense when the husband returns home (with or without their baby?), and it continues a motif of blocked views, especially through half-open doorways. The banisters are also fairly important throughout the movie. But noticing this shot is a good start, and I have yet to find another reviewer of the time who mentioned this or the other wordless sequences in the film.

In Ferguson's discussion of shooting the *Little Foxes* scene, there are two setups he doesn't include, and the angles on the carriage aren't quite right. His transcript of the dialogue, made from memory, doesn't completely correspond to that in the finished film, and some lines are spoken in different camera setups.

Colin Burnett provides a subtle analysis of Ferguson's multiple conceptions of realism and naturalism in "Going to the Theatre at the Movies:
Re-examining the Film Criticism of Otis Ferguson," in *Senses of Cinema*
(February 2004) at http://sensesofcinema.com/2004/feature-articles
/otis_ferguson.

4. James Agee: All There and Primed to Go Off

Nearly all the principal citations in the chapter can be identified in *JA*
from the movie title or the person mentioned. The exception is Agee's
remark on Hollywood as supreme in popular art (*JA*, 369). Agee's anonymous review of the novel *The Human Comedy* appeared as "The Pure in
Heart" in *Time*, 1 March 1943, 81, and is reprinted in Ashdown, *Complete
Journalism*, 490–91.

I've drawn two quotations from *Let Us Now Praise Famous Men* (Ballantine, 1960), 101, 93. The "illusion of embodiment" phrase is from p. 215.
Recently we've been given access to the limpid original, *Cotton Tenants:
Three Families* (Baffler / Melville House, 2013); I've drawn a quotation from
p. 202. Central to my understanding of Agee and Evans's enterprise is William Stott's brilliant *Documentary Expression and Thirties America* (Oxford,
1973). "Knoxville: Summer of 1915" is included, perhaps incorrectly, in
every edition of *A Death in the Family*. It originally appeared in *Partisan
Review* 5, no. 3 (August-September 1938): 22–25. Less often acknowledged
is Agee's lyrical introduction to Helen Levitt's book of photographs, *A
Way of Seeing* (Viking, 1965).

Agee's 1931 remembrance of I. A. Richards is in *Letters of James Agee to
Father Flye* (Bantam, 1963), 47; see also Laurence Bergreen's *James Agee:
A Life* (Dutton, 1984), 82–83. Agee's familiarity with new methods of literary analysis is further indicated in an unpublished 1941 *Time* review
of John Crowe Ransom's *The New Criticism* (New Directions, 1941). That
manuscript is reprinted in Ashdown, *Complete Journalism*, 603. It's hard
to doubt that he would have been in sympathy with Ransom's argument
that "the texture of poetry is incessant particularity" (*New Criticism*, 25).

Agee's corresponding skepticism about reflectionist accounts is
explained in more detail in some unpublished pieces gathered in Maland,
Complete Movie Reviews. Agee occasionally finds the dream analogy interesting, and he employs it in his "Suggestions to Librarian of Congress
Archibald MacLeish on Movies for Library of Congress Film Collection"
(1944). But he voices his suspicion of the sort of social-reflection accounts
offered by Kracauer and Deming. In "Notes on Movies and Reviewing

to Jean Kintner for a Museum of Modern Art Round Table" (c. 1949), he suggests that Hollywood decision makers are simply guessing at what appeals to an audience. The collective nature of that guesswork brings in so many disparate conceptions of life that what emerges on the screen could not plausibly reflect what "the public" thinks. "A movie does not grow out of The People; it is imposed on the people—as careful as possible a guess as to what they want. Moreover, the relative popularity or failure of a picture, though it means something, does not at all necessarily mean it has made a dream come true. It means, usually, just that something has been successfully imposed." Elsewhere Agee declares his commitment to treating cinema as an art, not a sociological phenomenon ("Notes for an Article on American Movies for Special Issue of *Horizon* on American Art," 1947).

For Agee's Hollywood-oriented scripts, see *Agee on Film: Five Film Scripts* (McDowell, Obolensky, 1960). The *Blue Hotel* extract is on p. 438. Huston's recollection of Agee's smile is in the preface, p. x. Agee's unrealized project for Chaplin, *The Tramp's New World*, is included in John Wranovics's study *Chaplin and Agee* (Palgrave Macmillan, 2005). My epigraph for this chapter, excerpted from a letter to Huston, comes from Wranovics's study, p. 91. The treatments for *The House* and *Man's Fate* are included in Robert Fitzgerald, *The Collected Short Prose of James Agee* (Calder and Boyars, 1972). Some unpublished treatments are included in Michael A. Lofaro and Hugh Davis, eds., *James Agee Rediscovered: The Journals of "Let Us Now Praise Famous Men" and Other New Manuscripts* (University of Tennessee Press, 2005). Here as well you can find the lacerating text, "America! Look at Your Shame!" On Agee's involvement with *Night of the Hunter*, see Jeffrey Couchman's *"The Night of the Hunter": A Biography of a Film* (Northwestern University Press, 2009).

No other American film critic has won so much attention. There are PhD dissertations on all aspects of his work, and scholars have brought out volumes of analysis, historical investigations, and detailed accounts of early drafts, unpublished manuscripts, and other primary documents. Agee, or his friends and family, apparently kept everything.

I have benefited enormously from Bergreen's *Agee: A Life*; Peter H. Ohlin's *Agee* (McDowell Obolensky, 1966); and Geneviève Moreau's *Restless Journey of James Agee*, trans. Miriam Kleiger and Morty Schiff (Morrow, 1977). See as well Neil Sinyard, "The Camera Eye of James Agee," in his *Filming Literature: The Art of Screen Adaptation* (Croom Helm, 1986), and Hugh Davis, *The Making of James Agee* (University of Tennessee Press, 2008). An excellent collection is *Agee at 100: Centennial Essays on the Works of James Agee* (University of Tennessee Press, 2012), which includes important primary research on Agee's film work by John Wranovics and Jeffrey Couchman.

Crucial to Agee's posthumous reputation are two Dwight Macdonald memoirs, the 1957 "James Agee," included in *Against the American Grain* (Random House, 1962), and the 1967 "Agee and the Movies," in *Dwight Macdonald on Movies* (Prentice-Hall, 1969). Macdonald's recollections are balanced by Robert Fitzgerald's memoir of the Harvard and Luce years in *Remembering James Agee*, ed. David Madden and Jeffrey J. Folks, 2nd ed. (University of Georgia Press, 1997), 37–88. Theodore Strauss's comment on Agee's style is in "No Jacks, No Giant-Killers," *Screen Writer* 1, no. 1 (June 1945): 8. I take Ezra Goodman's recollection of Agee as "an over-meticulous stylist" from his jaundiced *Fifty-Year Decline and Fall of Hollywood* (Simon and Schuster, 1961), 153.

James Naremore provides a sensitive appreciation of Agee's career in his recent collection, *An Invention without a Future: Essays in Cinema* (University of California Press, 2014), 247–63.

Although the 1960s canonized Agee as our finest film critic, his reputation has always been contested, probably most aggressively by his friend Manny Farber (see chapter 5). A plus-and-minus assessment is Phillip Lopate's "Agee's Gospel," published, with an irony its subject might appreciate, in *Nation*, 5 December 2005, 58–62.

A good overview of the press reactions to *Monsieur Verdoux*, both in America and abroad, can be found in Glenn Mitchell, *The Chaplin Encyclopedia* (Batsford, 1997), 191–98. Charles J. Maland provides a detailed account of United Artists' press campaign and the critical reaction in *Chaplin and American Culture: The Evolution of a Star Image* (Princeton University Press, 1989), 221–52. Eric Bentley's essay "*Monsieur Verdoux* and Theater" is included in his *In Search of Theater* (Vintage, 1953). Another influential discussion of the film that reflects the influence of New Criticism is Robert Warshow's 1947 piece "*Monsieur Verdoux*," included in *The Immediate Experience*, 177–91. Yet another contemporary review of interest comes from that reformed Surrealist J. B. Brunius in "Monsieur Verdoux," *Horizon*, March 1948, 166–78.

5. Manny Farber: Space Man

My epigraph comes from S. J. Perelman's satire on Farber and location-based movies, "Hell in the Gabardines," in *Keep It Crisp* (Random House, 1946), 3–14.

Principal quotations from Farber's film reviews not identified by movie title are as follows: On "non-theatrical" filming (*MF*, 143); the epigraph from 1977 (*MF*, 794); Ann Blyth's age (*MF*, 262); the burlesque (*MF*, 13); reading the book (*MF*, 227); Mondrian and plastic values (*MF*, 338); flattening the screen (*MF*, 340); truth of American life (*MF*, 384); snarling close-ups (*MF*, 386); "present-tense realism" (*MF*, 334).

Farber's art reviews remain uncollected. A bibliography is available in the catalog *Manny Farber* (Museum of Contemporary Art, Los Angeles, 1985), 69. I've drawn principally on his writing for two periodicals. Reviews in the *New Republic* include "Americans All," 2 February 1942, 146; "Thomas Benton's War," 20 April 1942, 542–43; "Scholars' Art," 11 May 1942, 645; "83-Year Tantrum," 31 January 1944, 155–56; "Mexican Master," 9 October 1944, 459–60; "Comic Strips," 4 September 1944, 279; and "Art for Science's Sake," 29 January 1945, 151–52. Other quotations come from the *Magazine of Art*: "Tchelitchew at Museum of Modern Art and Various Doings," December 1942, 202–5; "Artists for Victory," December 1942, 274–80; and "Feininger, Tack, and Burin," March 1943, 107–9. The passages on Milton Avery's color and Steig's drawing *Nerves* can be found in "Chaim Gross, Milton Avery, and William Steig," *Magazine of Art* 36 (January 1943): 204.

The Ferguson reference to "story, story, story" is in *OF*, 365.

Common Soldiers: A Self-Portrait and Other Portraits (Archer Press, 1979) by Janet Richards, Farber's first wife, includes recollections of their years in New York. Useful surveys of American abstraction and its context are Irving Sandler, *The Triumph of American Painting* (Praeger, 1970), and Dore Ashton, *The New York School: A Cultural Reckoning* (University of California Press, 1992, orig. 1972).

Clement Greenberg's "Towards a New Laocöon" is included in *The Collected Essays and Criticism*, vol. 1, *Perceptions and Judgments, 1939–1944*, ed. John O'Brian (University of Chicago Press, 1986), 23–38. My quotation about the necessary direction of pictorial art is from "Review of an Exhibition of André Masson," 99, and the observations on William Steig come from "Steig's Gallery: *The Lonely Ones*," 137–38, both from that same volume. On Greenberg, the standard biography is Florence Rubenfeld's *Clement Greenberg* (Scribner's, 1997); Greenberg's report on vanquishing Farber is on p. 82. ("He was so neurotic. He could've beaten me up.")

An extensive sampling of New York art world criticism of the period can be found in *Art in America, 1945–1970*, ed. Jed Perl (Library of America, 2014). The volume includes nothing by Farber.

On negative space, see Erle Loran, *Cézanne's Composition* (University of California Press, 1943). It's likely that Farber, a fervent admirer of Cézanne, knew the book. In the 1950 edition Loran thanks Hans Hofmann's lectures and writings for helping him formulate his ideas. Hofmann's teachings are condensed in *Search for the Real*, ed. Sarah T. Weeks and Bartlett H. Hayes Jr. (Addison Gallery, 1948). Both Farber and Greenberg surely knew Hofmann's ideas, which were circulating throughout the Manhattan gallery scene.

Over the years "negative space" has come to refer to what Loran calls negative *shape*—the way the areas not occupied by masses actively contribute to the composition. Negative shape is a two-dimensional product of the arrangement of the masses. For Loran, negative space proper creates plastic, three-dimensional relations, and Hofmann agrees: "Space discloses itself to us through volumes. 'Objects' are positive space. Negative space results from the relation of objects. Negative space is as concrete to the artist as is objective-positive space, and possesses an equal three dimensional effectiveness" (*Search for the Real*, 66–67). Farber's introduction to *Negative Space* would expand the term to indicate "the command of experience which an artist can set resonating through a film, a sense of terrain." Still, even this metaphorical broadening suggests not empty areas but dynamic relationships.

Farber's comments about Welles's dense, locked compositions find support in the recollections of one of the cinematographers who worked on *Othello*, which was begun in 1948. "It took a quarter of an hour to get the thing right, because Welles, maybe, wanted a tower in the distance to be seen between two strands of hair. Move a bit to the left, a bit to the right—and the actor had to be absolutely motionless, barely breathe." See Alberto Anile, *Orson Welles in Italy*, trans. Marcus Perryman (Indiana University Press, 2013), 165.

Farber's death in 2008 launched a wave of affectionate appreciation that has not subsided. Especially important is "The Adventure of Perception," two interviews with Kent Jones conducted by Eric Hynes on the occasion of a 2008 homage to Farber (http://blogs.indiewire.com/reverseshot/the_adventure_of_perception_a_conversation_about_manny_farber_with_kent_jones). See also Robert Walsh's introduction to the 1998 edition of *Negative Space* (Da Capo), ix–xii. Richard Corliss wrote a sparkling appraisal, "Termite of Genius," *Time*, 26 August 2008. More recently, a special issue of the online journal *Cinema Comparative Cinema* is devoted to Farber. Of special interest is the conversation between Jean-Pierre Gorin and Kent Jones, "The Law of the Frame." See www.ocec.eu/cinemacomparativecinema/pdf/ccc04/ccc04_eng.pdf.

This chapter has benefited from Donald Phelps's early and prescient appreciation, "Critic Going Everywhere," in *Covering Ground: Essays for Now* (Croton, 1969), 115–21. Phelps's little magazine, *For Now*, published a Farber collection in issue no. 9 (1968); several of his art reviews are included. Farber's unattributed borrowing from Ferguson's *Kane* essay is discussed by Colin Burnett in "Silence Is Golden: The Ferguson-Farber Affair," *Synoptique*, 16 April 2004, available at www.synoptique.ca/core /en/archived_articles/burnett_silence. We also have James Naremore's compact, discerning essay on Farber in *An Invention without a Future: Essays on Cinema* (University of California Press, 2014), 264–74.

The history of deep-focus cinematography, with some emphasis on the 1940s, is considered in chapter 27 of David Bordwell, Janet Staiger, and Kristin Thompson, *The Classical Hollywood Cinema: Film Style and Mode of Production to 1960* (Columbia University Press, 1985), as well as in my *On the History of Film Style* (Harvard University Press, 1997) and *Figures Traced in Light: On Cinematic Staging* (University of California Press, 2005). My essay "William Cameron Menzies: One Forceful, Impressive Idea," is available at www.davidbordwell.net. See also Patrick Keating, *Hollywood Lighting from the Silent Era to Film Noir* (Columbia University Press, 2009).

6. Parker Tyler: A Suave and Wary Guest

Iris Barry's remark, which I use as the chapter's epigraph, is in the introduction to the first edition of *The Hollywood Hallucination* (Creative Arts, 1944), vii.

Because Tyler elaborated his ideas in books, much of my discussion summarizes entire chapters. Principal quotations not identified by movie title: On Veronica Lake as wraith (*MM*, 84); on Sinatra (*MM*, 5); on Chaplin (*CC*, 31); on Hollywood's vitality (*MM*, ix); on the film as a three-ring circus (*HH*, 15); on crevices (*MM*, xiv); on the Single Instance (*HH*, 37–46); on artifice (*HH*, 72–73); on *A Woman's Face* (*HH*, 35); on the charade of voices (*MM*, 1–30); on young actors as cannon fodder (*MM*, 151–52); on Good Villains and Bad Heroes (*HH*, chap. 5); on women's roles (*HH*, chap. 4); on myth generally (*MM*, xvii–xxix); on the infantile logic of the charade (*HH*, 177); on Verdoux as the start of the Chaplin saga (*CC*, 179); on being a suave and wary guest (*HH*, 36); on the mother and the homosexual son (*MM*, 97).

The opening of *The Young and Evil* comes from the Olympia Press edition of 1960.

Neal Pearson offers a detailed publication history of the novel, along with a biography of Charles Henri Ford, in "The Beginning of Gay Lit: Charles Henri Ford and Parker Tyler," at www.nealpearsonrarebooks.com. Tyler recalls Ford and their "naughty novel" in his massive biography *The Divine Comedy of Pavel Tchelitchew* (Fleet, 1967). Tyler's anthology *Modern Things* is from Galleon Press (1934), and the poems "Hollywood Dream Suite" and "Address to My Mother" are on pp. 85–86.

My synopsis of *Myra Breckinridge* is not exactly straight, so to speak, but I tried to avoid spoilers. The tribute to Tyler is on p. 14 of the 1968 Little, Brown edition.

The crack about Tyler's style comes from D. Mosdell's review of *Magic and Myth of the Movies* in *Canadian Forum* 27 (August 1947): 118. "Hollywood's Terror Films" and "Portrait in Film," Kracauer's review of *Chaplin: Last of the Clowns*, are reprinted in *Siegfried Kracauer's American Writings: Essays on Film and Popular Culture*, ed. Johannes von Moltke and Kristy Rawson (University of California Press, 2012), 41–46 and 188–190. For further information on the relationship between the critics see Adrian Martin, "The Dream Team: The Parker Tyler and Siegfried Kracauer Correspondence," *Cineaste* 40, no. 1 (Winter 2014): 20–25.

Richard Maltby offers his own treatment of the Single Instance in "'A Brief Romantic Interlude': Dick and Jane Go to 3½ Seconds of the Classical Hollywood Cinema," in *Post-Theory: Reconstructing Film Studies*, ed. David Bordwell and Noël Carroll (University of Wisconsin Press, 1996), 434–59.

Tyler asked Henry Miller to write the preface to *The Hollywood Hallucination*, but the publishers wisely rejected it. The text, in which Miller gets the title of Tyler's book wrong, is still worth seeking out as a rant. See "Original Preface to 'Hollywood's Hallucination,'" in *Sunday After the War* (New Directions, 1944), 39–56.

In support of my suggestion that there are affinities between Kenneth Burke and Parker Tyler, I'd invoke the title essay in Burke's *Philosophy of Literary Form* (Louisiana State University Press, 1941), 1–137. A good overview of trends in literary criticism of the period is Stanley Edgar Hyman, *The Armed Vision* (Knopf, 1948).

Deming's critique of Tyler's social irresponsibility comes in "The Close-up of Love," *Partisan Review* 12, no. 3 (Summer 1945): 393. Her *Running Away from Myself: A Dream Portrait of America Drawn from Films of the Forties* (Grossman, 1969) was finished in 1950 but remained unpublished until 1969. For an account of Deming's work, see Albert Moran's "A Poetics of Film-Audience Reception? Barbara Deming Goes to the Movies," in *Watching Films: New Perspectives on Movie Going, Exhibition, and Reception*, ed. Karina Aveyard and Albert Moran (Intellect, 2013), 55–68.

I discuss the tradition of symptomatic interpretation in *Making Meaning: Inference and Rhetoric in the Interpretation of Cinema* (Harvard University Press, 1989). I've registered my reservations about reflection-based interpretations in chapter 1 of *Poetics of Cinema* (Routledge, 2007).

7. Afterlives

I'm grateful to Judith Noble for information about Tyler's relation to Maya Deren. Thanks as well to Christophe Gauthier for information about screenings at postwar French ciné-clubs, and to Kelley Conway for acting as liaison.

Farber's painting career is covered in two catalogs: *Manny Farber* (Museum of Contemporary Art, Los Angeles, 1985) and *Manny Farber: About Face* (Museum of Contemporary Art, San Diego, 2003). Both include biographical information, and several essays in each volume discuss the relation of Farber's painting to his film criticism. See also Jonathan Rosenbaum's 1983 essay "Thinking about (Personal) History Lessons: The Movie Paintings of Manny Farber," in the online journal *Rouge* 12.

Cahiers du Cinéma published an extensive interview with Farber in special number 334–35 (April 1982): 54–65, 130. The online journal *Rouge* published a Farber dossier in 2009, which included the Donald Phelps essay I mention above as well as memoirs and appreciations and a Farber piece on late-night radio.

Tyler's early ideas about European imports and the American avant-garde are drawn from "Movie Letter: Lament for the Audience—and a Mild Bravo," *Kenyon Review* 12, no. 4 (Autumn 1950): 689–96. Thanks to the Internet, you can listen to a precious recording of a 1953 panel discussion on "Poetry and the Film," which brought together Tyler, Deren, and others, including a boorish Dylan Thomas, at Amos Vogel's Cinema 16. A transcript is on Paul Cronin's site *The Sticking Place*. P. Adams Sitney discusses the trance-film trend in the avant-garde in *Visionary Film: The American Avant-Garde*, 3rd ed. (Oxford University Press, 2002), chaps. 1–5.

Agee reviewed a 1946 program of Maya Deren's films, and she replied with a letter to the *Nation*. She also answered Manny Farber's critique in the *New Republic*. See *The Legend of Maya Deren: A Documentary Biography and Collected Works*, vol. 1, pt. 2, "Chambers (1942–1947)," ed. Catrina Neiman (Anthology Film Archive, 1988), 382–85, 410–17. Farber took another dig a few years later, when he noted that the bandit's sword in *Rashomon* "somehow rises (Maya Deren-fashion) as if it had just had a big meal of sex hormones" (*MF*, 377). In 1956, Deren talked back to Farber's essay "The Gimp": "Mr. Farber is not writing a criticism of *Citizen Kane*. He is having a tantrum." See Maya Deren, "The *Village Voice* Pieces," *Film Culture*, no. 39 (Winter 1965): 46–49.

See Claude-Edmonde Magny, *The Age of the American Novel: The Film Aesthetic of Fiction between the Two Wars*, trans. Eleanor Hochman (Ungar, 1972). The Pierre Bailly essay, "Avis aux usagers du plan fixe," is in *Gazette du Cinéma*, no. 4 (October 1950): 7. The Bazin essays I'm alluding to are "La technique du *Citizen Kane*," *Les Temps Modernes* 2, no. 17 (1947): 943–49; "William Wyler, or the Jansenist of Directing," *Bazin at Work: Major Essays and Reviews from the Forties and Fifties*, ed. Bert Cardullo (Routledge, 1997; orig. 1948), 1–22; and *Orson Welles: A Critical View*, trans. Jonathan Rosenbaum (Harper and Row, 1978; orig. 1950). For more on French stylistic analysis of the period, see the third chapter of my *On the History of Film Style* (Harvard University Press, 1997).

Index

Page numbers in italics refer to illustrations.

Visconti, Luchino, 137
von Stroheim, Erich, 26

Wallace, Henry, 102
Wallis, Hal, 142
Walsh, Raoul, 61, 83, 104, 134, 139, 140, 142
Warhol, Andy, 112, 136
Warren, Robert Penn, 32
Watts, Richard, Jr., 43
Wavelength, 137
Ways of Love, 137
Webb, Clifton, 142
Weber, Max, 85
Weinberg, Herman G., 3
Welles, Orson, 31, 47, 52, 53, 97, 123, 142; Agee on, 61; composition, 99, *100*, 101; long static shot, 141
Wellman, William, 69, 142
West, Mae, 121, 123
Weston, Jessie, *From Ritual to Romance*, 116
We Were Strangers, 78, *80*, 94, 105
What Price Glory?, 104
White Cliffs of Dover, The, 26, 61
White Elephant directors, 110, 138, 139
White Tower, 104
Wieland, Joyce, 138

Wild Bunch, The, 139
Wilde, Oscar, 122, 126
Wilder, Billy, 61, 74, 142
Wilder, Thornton, *Our Town*, 24
Wild Strawberries, 135
Wilson, 61
Wilson, Edmund, 20, 21
With the Marines at Tarawa, 68
Wolfe, Thomas, *Look Homeward, Angel*, 60
Wolfenstein, Martha, 116, 117, 123
Woman of Paris, A, 128
Woman's Face, A, 120
Woolf, Virginia, 24, 30, 149
Wordsworth, William, 62
Wyler, William, 6, 47, 54, 81, 104, 142

Yearling, The, 140
Yellow Jack, 36
Young, Robert, 70
Young, Stark, 41, 42, 43, 70, 151–52
Young, Vernon, 3
Young and the Evil, The (Parker Tyler and Charles Henri Ford), 111
Youth Runs Wild, 95

Zanuck, Darryl F., 142
Zéro de Conduite, 69